W9-BSD-895

Shut Up,
Stop Whining,
and
Get a Life

Shut Up, Stop Whining, and Get a Life

A Kick-Butt Approach to a Better Life

LARRY WINGET

WILEY

John Wiley & Sons, Inc.

Published by John Wiley & Sons, Inc., Hoboken, New Jersey.
Published simultaneously in Canada.

For general information on our other products and services please contact our Customer Care
Department within the United States at (800) 762-2974, outside the United States at (317) 572-
3993 or fax (317) 572-4002.

Designations used by companies to distinguish their products are often claimed by trademarks. In
all instances where the author or publisher is aware of a claim, the product names appear in Initial
Capital letters. Readers, however, should contact the appropriate companies for more complete
information regarding trademarks and registration.

Wiley also publishes its books in a variety of electronic formats. Some content that appears in print
may not be available in electronic books. For more information about Wiley products, visit our web
site at www.wiley.com.

Library of Congress Cataloging-in-Publications Data:
Winget, Larry.
    Shut up, stop whining, and get a life : a kick-butt approach to a better life / Larry Winget.
        p. cm.
    ISBN 0-471-65465-5 (cloth)
1. Life skills—Handbooks, manuals, etc. 2. Conduct of life. 3. Success. I. Title.
    HQ2037.W57 2004
646.7—dc22

2004005529

Printed in the United States of America.

10 9 8 7 6 5 4

I lovingly dedicate this book to all of the crap that ever happened to me. It has made me what I am. It caused me to read, to search, to pay attention, to learn, to detach, to accept, to gain perspective, and to create the life I have always wanted.

Without all of the crap that ever happened to me, I would be like 99.9 percent of the world: leading a life of mediocrity, full of blame, resentment, and whining.

I needed the crap to happen to me because without it, there would be no book for you to read and you would have no reason to listen to me.

So for every crappy thing that ever happened to me, I give thanks!

Contents

Preface ix

Acknowledgments xv

About the Author xvii

Before You Start xix

Chapter 1   Shut Up!   1

Chapter 2   Stop Whining!   9

Chapter 3   Get a Life!   18

Chapter 4   How to Live by Design, Not by Default   28

Chapter 5   Slaughtering the Sacred Self-Help Cows   42

Chapter 6   Your Beliefs Determine Your Outcome   61

Chapter 7   The Enjoyment Factor   66

Chapter 8   Fitness, Fatness, and More   77

Chapter 9   Everyone Screws Up   92

Chapter 10   Religion Versus Spirituality: Whose Side Is God On?   98

Chapter 11   Get Smarter   107

Chapter 12   Stress: Who Needs It?   114

Chapter 13   Learn to Relax   117

Chapter 14   Money Rules!   119

Chapter 15   Relationships—Friendship, Marriage, and Other Calamities   135

Chapter 16   Kids Are a Pain in the Butt   170

Chapter 17   Sex: You Gotta Love It   178

Chapter 18   Love Is the Key   183

Chapter 19   Criticism Happens   187

Chapter 20   The More You Give the More You Get   193

Chapter 21   Sometimes Work Is Just Plain Work   197

Chapter 22   You Are Out of Time   207

Chapter 23   Success Is a Balancing Act   212

Chapter 24   Give Up Hope   214

Chapter 25   Guilt Serves No Purpose   216

Chapter 26   Worry Is a Waste of Time   217

Chapter 27   Selfishness Is a Good Thing   219

Chapter 28   A Deal Is a Deal   221

Chapter 29   Hard Lessons to Learn   223

Chapter 30   The Test for Success   225

Chapter 31   A Final Thought   228

Preface

This book is tough. It is meant to be. It is written that way because I want to shake you up and wake you up. I want to make you mad. I want to make you sick of accepting less than the best for yourself. I want you to become disgusted with your life and I want to create in you an intense desire to have more, do more and most of all, become more. I want you to see you can create the life you want. I want you to have it all. But in order to do that I may have to kick your butt and tick you off a little along the way.

For some of you the approach may seem harsh, but some of you will barely be disturbed. It just depends on where you are in your life. If someone is deeply asleep, sometimes you have to shake that person very hard to make him fully awake. If he is just dozing, a little nudge is enough. For some of you this book will be your nudge. For others, it will be a rude awakening—a slap in the face.

My style is confrontational. However, my confrontational style by itself would only make you mad. Now let us get clear on this: I am not afraid of making you mad. In fact, I enjoy that a bit. Because if you get a little mad, that means you are willing to be challenged. And while you are being challenged, you can consider my suggestions for how to live a better life. Hopefully you will find me not only confrontational, but also supportive. I want you to feel supported because that is my motive. While the style of writing is confrontational and in-your-face, my motive is to give you the courage to accomplish whatever you want in life.

This book is not like the other self-help books you have read. The market would not tolerate this kind of abuse as a rule. I think most of the books on the market today just help people suffer in comfort. They are a pacifier for the most part. They want you to believe that regardless of how much your life sucks, that is okay; there are plenty of conditions that were beyond your control that led you to that condition. Those books sometimes do nothing but help you coat yourself in a shell that serves no purpose except to make it harder for the real truth—I mean the *ugly* truth—to get in. My goal is not to help you suffer in comfort. My goal is to break through that shell to offer you some truths that will change your perspective, make you think, and alter your results. The way I do that is by getting in your face and shaking you up a bit in order to wake you up from the sleep of mediocrity.

It is pretty much like the mule and the two-by-four theory: You have to get the mule's attention first with the two-by-four in order to get him to do something. Consider this book to be the two-by-four in your life.

> **"I don't give them hell, I just tell the truth and they think it is hell."**
>
> **—Harry S. Truman**

I do not want to mislead you by seeming to be high and mighty or by pretending to have mastered the truth. I have not mastered all of what I talk about in these pages. Unlike others who write books and give speeches saying they have mastered all they speak of and write about, I would rather be honest and just tell you I am a mess like everyone else in this world. I am just doing the best I can with what I have learned until I can learn a little more and then do a little better. Actually that is all I am suggesting you do as well. Learn a little from this writing and do the best you can with it until you learn a little more and can do a little better.

I am still learning. I do not know it all. There was a time not so long ago when I did think that I knew it all. That was just plain stupid. Now I know that the more you really do know, the more you realize you do not know.

Therefore, I openly admit to you right now I do not know everything there is to know about being successful or getting rich or being healthy or anything else, really.

This book is not about what I do not know; it is about what I do know. I am absolutely sure of the things in this book. The things I talk about in this book are the result of thousands of hours spent reading thousands of books and listening to instructional audiotapes, and many years of gaining personal experience by living life the hard way—by screwing up and every once in a while, doing things right as well. This is real world stuff. This stuff works. I know it does.

I have written this book for you. Maybe just for you. At least you are the one who is reading it right now. You are here because you need to be here. Either you bought it, or someone gave it to you, or you stole it. The bottom line is, here you are, book in hand, ready to get going. Take advantage of this time with me. Let me rough you up a little bit. Let me tell you the truth as I have discovered it. Let me show you a way to get what you want out of life. You deserve it. So read the book and do what it says. Then celebrate your success!

"There are no rules here. We're just trying to accomplish something."

—Thomas Edison

> "Truth is often uncomfortable. It is only comforting to those who do not wish to ignore it. Then, truth becomes not only comforting, but inspiring."
> —Neale Donald Walsch,
> *Conversations with God*, Book 3

By the way, that is really what Truth does. Truth does not exist to support your comfort zone. Truth exists to shatter your comfort zone and move you closer to your True Purpose.

Warning! Cliché ahead: "The truth hurts."

Heard that before? It is true. Some clichés are. In fact, this little cliché is the way I have begun to measure the truth: if it hurts, it is probably the truth. So since this book contains the truth, it will probably hurt. And if it does hurt, then you will know that for you at least, it is the truth.

Another cliché I bet you have heard: "The truth will set you free."

Another oldie but goodie—in fact, it is Biblical (John 8:32 KJV). And while true, I consider it incomplete.

"What? You are going to try to improve on the Bible?"

Face it, the Bible was written a couple of thousand years ago and we have learned a few things since then, so some literary license is completely acceptable in my opinion. Let me give you another quotation that adds to that famous Biblical statement and, in my opinion, completes the thought:

> "The truth will set you free, but first it will piss you off."
> —Werner Erhard

That is what this book will do to you. (In fact, maybe it already has.) However:

"**All human unhappiness comes from not facing reality squarely, exactly as it is.**"

—**Buddha**

Acknowledgments

Thanks to the writers whose works have most influenced my life and this work: Wayne Dyer, Deepak Chopra, Marianne Williamson, Louise Hay, Kennedy Shultz, Thomas Moore, Paramahansa Yogananda, Neale Donald Walsch, and all the many others whose books I have loved and learned from.

Thanks to the people who have personally helped me in so many ways not only during the writing of this book but through the painful growth that took place over many years in order for me to write it.

To my wife, Rose Mary, who has had to put up with more than any person should ever have to put up with in order to learn how to be in a relationship with me. I am not an easy person to live with or be with—I know that and so does everyone who knows me—but she knows and understands that better than anyone. She deserves a prize for putting up with me, my eccentricities, my rage, my passions, my energy, my intolerance, my silliness, my boundless ego, my noise, and my stuff. Bless her.

To my boys, Tyler and Patrick. No two siblings could be as different as they and yet similar in so many ways as well. They have given me a ride on a rollercoaster of emotions that I would not trade for anything. I am proud of them in every way and grateful to them for becoming men who are my two best friends.

To my friends, and there are not many. This includes my speaker buddies and the other few personal friends I have, as well as some other individuals who appeared quite anonymously along the way to guide me when I needed help, and gave me encouragement and chastisement. Each helped me more than I can ever say in their unique and different way.

To Keppler Associates, Inc. This great team of people understands what I do and keeps me on the road in front of people so I can do it. They are fun to work with—true professionals—and keep my calendar full and the money coming in.

Special thanks to Vic Osteen, my marketing director, my associate, my business partner, and most of all my trusted friend who takes care of me, looks out for me, and keeps the business running profitably while I am not around. Thanks Vic, I could not do any of it without your stability. You are my best bud.

About the Author

Larry Winget is known as the Pitbull of Personal Development® and The World's Only Irritational Speaker.® He is edgy. Controversial. Cantankerous. Antagonistic. Sarcastic. Opinionated. Caustic. Direct. In-your-face. He is definitely one of a kind.

He is a philosopher of success who just happens to be hilarious. He teaches universal principles that will work for anyone, in any business, at any time. He believes that most of us have complicated life way too much and take it way too seriously.

As one of the busiest professional speakers working today, Larry is in high demand speaking to groups, associations and corporations around the world about his philosophy of success through service and the power of taking personal responsibility.

He does not mince words—not in his speaking or in his writing. He delivers the cold, ugly truth in a way that is provocative, interesting, and funny.

He delivers truth full of humor and humor full of truth. And he is anything but boring!

Before You Start

Do not even think about beginning this book without a highlighter and a pen handy. There is a lot of good stuff in this book and you are going to want to highlight things to refer to again later. I encourage you to make notes in the margins and fill in all the forms and to write in the book all you want. It is your book for your private use and you should use it not only as a reference book but also as a workbook.

If you are going to use quotes from this book either in your own writing or speaking or if you want to share what I have said in this book with others, then remember: I said this stuff. Give me credit. If I did not say it, then I have given credit to the person who did. If you quote them, give them credit. If you write a book and I quote you, then I will give you credit. Is that a deal?

Do not share this book. If you think it is good enough you want your friend to read it, then buy her a copy. By the time you finish the book it should be marked up and written in anyway, and that will make it too personal to share with anyone else. Besides it is just tacky to give someone a used book that has been written in. If you think you are going to loan your book to someone who should read it, expecting to have it returned, then you are truly naive. (Besides, how am I going to make any money if you give away your book? Buy another one or two or even a case to share with those who need to shut up and stop whining.)

If you do not like the book, then please do not feel compelled to share that with me. I do not care. Seriously, I do not. I am not interested in your criticism or your ideas or your feedback. And do not think I am going to give you a refund just because you do not like the book. That will not happen no matter how much you hate it or how unhappy you are with what I have said, or me. However, if you do like the book, then please send me a note or an e-mail to let me know. I appreciate hearing nice things from people.

"You must speak straight so that your words may go as sunlight into our hearts."

—Cochise, Chiricahua Chief

Shut Up,
Stop Whining,
and
Get a Life

CHAPTER 1

Shut Up!

"What? You just told me to shut up?"

Yes, I sure did. Someone needs to. If you are like most of the people in the world you are probably talking so much you cannot even hear what is being said. My dad always put it this way: "You are broadcasting when you ought to be tuned in." In other words, shut your mouth for a minute and pay attention.

That has probably been your biggest problem. You were so busy talking you did not shut up long enough to pay attention. You missed all the important lessons of life.

> **"Most of us are so busy running around creating the soap opera and drama we call our lives that we don't hear anything."**
>
> **—Louise Hay**

In the New Testament there is a story about Jesus, traveling in a fishing boat with his disciples. A big wind comes up, the waves rise, and all of the disciples think they're going to die. They awaken Jesus from his nap, whining and crying, and he says, "Hush, be still" (Mark 4:39 KJV). Then he goes on to talk to them about their faith. (But he first has to make the winds, the waves, and the disciples hush.)

When I was growing up, I was often told to "Hush!" I knew exactly what it meant. In fact, the word "hush" has been shortened to "shhhh." (I bet you did not know that, did you? See, you are already learning stuff.) When you hear "hush" or "shhhh" you know it means to be quiet. Actually I think if those words of Jesus were being translated today, they could just as easily be, "Shut up! Be quiet! I'm about to teach you something."

That is what I am saying to you here. Shut up! I am about to teach you something.

Shut Up and Listen

It is impossible to listen while you are talking. It just cannot be done. Yet all of the good information comes to us only when we are quiet and listen. You cannot learn while you are talking. You can only learn when you are listening. So when was the last time you really got quiet and listened? I mean really listened? You should try it some time. You might be amazed at what you hear. Jimi Hendrix once said, "Knowledge speaks but wisdom listens."

LISTEN TO OTHERS

Stop and listen to your spouse or significant other. I do not mean the kind of listening you do when the TV is blaring in the background. I mean the kind of listening where you stop and hold hands and look into each other's eyes and really listen. This special exchange will take you to new heights in your relationship.

Take some time to listen to your kids. I once read that the average parent spends less than seven minutes a day in direct communication with their children. I know how hard it is to communicate with your kids. I have been there. Especially when you are the parent of a teenager. Sometimes, the last thing your teenager wants to do is talk to you. Usually it is just easier not to talk to them because all they do is make monosyllabic grunts in response to you. Tough. Make them talk. Bug the hell out of them and force the communication if you have to. Both of my sons went through periods when they hated talking to me. How sad for them. I just kept talking and forced them to listen. I made them talk and forced myself to listen, even when what they had to say was hard for me to listen to. For instance, one time my son, Tyler, told me I ought to listen to my own speech. Ouch!

Most people think communication is about talking. That is only a small part of it. Listening is the biggest part. Become very good at it with those you love.

LISTEN TO YOUR CUSTOMERS

Earl Nightingale said, "All of the money you are ever going to have is currently in the hands of someone else." In business, we call that "someone else" the customer. They have the money. They share it with us when we serve them well. One of the ways you serve your customers well is by listening to them.

You might be saying you do not really have customers, but we all have customers. You might not call them customers, but you still have them. You might call them patients, clients, co-workers or the audience, but they are still your customers. Listen to them. They have all of the information necessary for you to serve them, solve their problems, and make them happy. Do those things and you will be rewarded.

LISTEN TO THOSE WHO KNOW MORE THAN YOU DO

Someone knows more than you do. That may be hard for you to believe but it is true. And some of those who know more than you will share that information. Find them. Ask for their help. Do you know what will happen as a result of asking? They will help. No kidding. Most people who have made it are more than willing to help others, but most people do not genuinely ask for help. Instead they whine about how it is. That is much different than a sincere request for information. Very few ask and even fewer do what they are advised. Do not be like that. When you ask, really take the advice that is offered. After all, you are asking someone who knows more than you. Do not waste the exchange.

By the way, do you want to know how to find out if other people know more than you do? Look at their results. Results never lie. If their results are better than yours, then they know something you do not know. Or maybe they are just willing to do more than you are willing to do. In any case, pay attention.

Spend some time with those who are doing better than you. Watch them. Listen to them. Figure out what they are doing and then go do it yourself. If you duplicate their effort, then you will duplicate their results. As my friend Joe Charbonneau said, "Do what the masters do and you will become a master."

LISTEN TO THE EXPERTS

Great speakers, teachers, philosophers, and books are available on audiotape or compact disc—and many are now even available as e-downloads on your computer via various web sites. My best teachers have come to me through audiotapes. And the best thing is that it is just so convenient. Through audiotapes and CDs, my mentors show up on my schedule. I can listen in my car, on an airplane, in my office, or lying by the pool. I heard once that during our lifetime the amount of time spent in our car is the same amount of time it takes to earn the equivalent of four PhD programs. You can use that windshield time to learn how to do almost anything: become rich, more successful, a better leader, or a more effective parent. You name it and I bet there is an audio program available on it. You can even learn how to lose weight by listening to audiotapes—although the best way to lose weight is to stop putting so much food in your mouth!

I have thousands of dollars invested in my audio library. It is one of my most prized possessions. I am convinced that my audio library has had a bigger influence on my life than any other educational source.

LISTEN TO GREAT MUSIC

I have a problem with total silence. I wish that were not the case. I would love to be able to sit in total silence and just meditate. I have friends who can do that and they say it is wonderful. Not me, I just cannot do it. So I have learned to listen to meditative music—music that can relax me, music that can inspire me. Some of it causes my mind to become creative. Some of it causes me to become sleepy. Some of it just makes me smile.

Go to a good music store and visit the new age and classical sections. Pick some good instrumental music; put it on the stereo and chill.

I am not asking you to give up your other favorite music. It serves a purpose too. No one should ever ask me to give up Leon Russell, Elvis, Merle Haggard, Willie Nelson, Van Morrison, or the really good rock-n-roll from the 1950s, 1960s and early 1970s. It is not going to happen. The blues, classical, rock, country, new age, big band (but not rap, I hate that stuff) all serve a purpose and I enjoy listening to most of it. Listen to only good music and learn to enjoy it for different reasons.

LISTEN TO YOUR SELF

Notice I did not say "yourself." I said "your Self." I do not mean you should talk to yourself and listen to it—although you do that all the time. I am talking about listening to your higher Self. The "better you" that knows what you ought to be doing. You might call it your conscience. You might call it your "gut." I do not care what you call it; I just want you to listen to it. It is smarter than you are. It is tuned in at higher levels than you are. It knows! So listen to it. You also might try doing what it says.

LISTEN TO GOD

By the way, that "Higher Self" I was just talking about—that was God. Really. Some folks are not comfortable thinking they might actually have a direct link to God like that. But you do. That Inner Voice—the smart one, the one that likes you, knows what to do, and wants the best for you—that one is God. It is in every one of us. The problem is we do not listen to it. We listen to the other voice. The one that is full of doubt. That one is not God. That one is you.

SOMETIMES, YOU SHOULD NOT LISTEN

"Wait, first you say to listen and now you are telling me not to listen. Make up your mind. So are there really things I should not listen to?"

Yes. Just like there is a list of things and people you should listen to, there is also a list of things and people you should not listen to:

- Do not listen to someone who is broke tell you how to be rich.
- Do not listen to a fat doctor who smokes tell you what it takes to be healthy.
- Do not listen to someone tell you how to be successful when they are not.
- Do not listen to a preacher tell you that you are worthless sinner.
- Do not listen to people who talk bad about other people.
- Do not listen to office gossip.
- Do not listen to anyone put you down for any reason at any time.
- Do not listen to yourself when you are talking bad about yourself.

This one needs additional explanation. I know I told you to listen to your Self. That is true. But be very careful when you listen to yourself. No one will ever talk as badly about you or to you as you will to yourself. Do your best to control that negative self-talk. When you catch yourself saying things like "I could never do that" or "I'm not good at that" or "I'm so stupid"—STOP! Regroup and restate what you should be saying to yourself: "I can do this!" and things that move you closer to the result you want, not further from it.

"I get it. Some of this is stuff I already know. So far, not much new information here. When do we get to the good stuff? What's next?"

Are you ready for the good stuff? I am almost there. But we have to lay some groundwork first. Do not worry. It is about to get ugly. I will not disappoint you.

So what is next? Easy. Stop whining.

CHAPTER 2

Stop Whining!

Whining is everywhere. Open your ears and you will hear it in every restaurant, at the supermarket, on television, on the radio, in your workplace, in your home, and even inside your own head or coming out of your own mouth.

We have even made whining the number one entertainment program in the world today. Have you ever watched *Jerry Springer*? Do not try to deny it. I ask that question in my speeches and no one ever admits it. It did not become one of the world's number one-rated television programs by people *not* watching it. So you have seen it.

The show amazes me. It is about people who will not take responsibility for their circumstances and are on the show just to whine. You will see some guy on there who is totally confused by the fact that both his wife and his girlfriend are leaving him. He just cannot figure out how that could happen. Well, let me see. You are fat, ugly, and stupid; you have tattoos from head to toe and only have three teeth. Get a clue!

Very few of us are willing to take responsibility for what is happening in our life. Why should we? No one is really asking us to.

People are becoming more and more tolerant of the whiners. It is so commonplace we hardly notice it any more.

Not me. I notice. And it makes me sick. What I find is the whiners, if you can get them to shut up for a minute, are also sick of whining. They are whining to get attention and they really want someone to grab them and tell them to shut up, stop whining, and get a life!

So if you are a whiner, and we all are from time to time, I believe you are sick of it and are ready for things to change. You are sick of not doing well; sick of the failures; sick of being broke; sick of the lousy relationships; sick and tired of being sick and tired; just plain sick of it all.

If you are unhappy, unsuccessful, sick or broke—please just keep it to yourself. The rest of us do not want or need to hear about it, so do not feel compelled to share!

The following letter is a prime example of the kind of whining I am talking about. It is a real letter that was sent to me by a "fan." I have not changed one word of it—not the punctuation, not the spelling, and not the whining.

Dear Mr. Winget,

   I hope you can find time in your busy schedule to read my letter. I am so troubled, I truly wish you can help. I will try to make this as brief as possible. I am a thirty-six year old hairstylist. I am single, and my life is so painful. I really do not know who to turn to. My dream in life is to have a successful career doing something I enjoy. But my biggest dream in life is to get married and have a family. And that dream has just been shattered. I met and fell in love with the girl of my dreams. It was heaven sent, we both thought the world of each other. But she decided we were moving too fast and she left me. I am completely devastated and heartbroken. We had both told each other that we were perfect for each other. Now I am alone. My second problem is my career. Throughout my life growing up I was brought up to be a pro baseball player by my parents. They never taught me the importance of school, as long as I could hit homeruns. Well I barely graduated high school. That summer I had tryouts with two professional teams. I did not make either team. Now I was lost. I had to take any job I could. For years I always thought I was going to be a star in the major leagues. I never gave any other career a thought. I decided to become a hairstylist. Schooling was only a year, and I would have a career. I never really had it in my heart to be a hairstylist. Now fifteen years later I am miserable. I do not want to be a hairstylist any more. This depresses me everyday. I would love to have a career helping people not end up like me. Help them set goals and help them obtain them. How do I get a career like that? My third problem is that I am in major financial debt. I just recently filed for bankruptcy. I had a major gambling problem, which is now under control. This is so difficult for me I feel so trapped. I want to change careers, settle down and get married. But with my financial problem I cannot do either. Please I would truly appreciate any advice you could share with me. I am heartbroken, broke and confused.

Thank you sincerely,

Joe Bob Whiner (Not his real name but it should be.)

Are you sick yet? Is it any wonder his girlfriend left him? When I read this letter I nearly threw up! Want to know what my advice was? "Shut up, stop whining, and get a life!" I wrote this guy back and told him I had never read such a pitiful pile of drivel in my life. I told him that he was sickening to himself and to everyone around him and now to me; I asked how could he be surprised by his crummy life when his outlook on life was so crummy. Then I went on to explain in detail what was wrong and what he could do to fix his life. I gave him the condensed version of this book (you are getting the whole load). But the message is the same. By the way, about six weeks later the guy wrote me another letter thanking me for being the only person who ever told him to quit whining and get on with his life. The other responses he received were "nice" and commiserated with him about how sad it all was. He said my response had changed his direction and he was making major improvements. However, the really sad thing is that this letter is pretty typical of what is going on in our society.

It Is Everyone's Fault but Mine

We have become a society of victims. Tune in the television to the talk shows and listen to all of those pitiful people blame others for their problems. *Jerry Springer, Maury, Montel, Ricki,* and all the rest are full of whining blamers. Is it not amazing how these people can blame everyone except themselves for their problems?

I am sick of parents blaming the violence on television as the reason their kid just blew up the neighbor's dog or for school shootings. Violence on television and in the movies is too prevalent—I will give you that. And I will also agree that many people are susceptible to what they see or listen to. But lousy parenting is the real cause of messed up kids.

I am sick of listening to people blame their lousy life on the fact they have ADHD (attention deficit/hyperactivity disorder), or they were first-born, or they were breast-fed or bottle-fed. I am tired of people blaming and then suing bartenders because they do not know when to stop drinking, and then they go out and smash into another car and kill someone.

I am sick of people blaming and then suing cigarette companies because they are dying of cancer. Didn't they know cigarettes are not good for them? Let me see, the concept is that you set something on fire and then you suck that fire down into your lungs. Did they really think that was the purpose of lungs? If they are really that stupid then they deserve their problem.

I am sick and tired of listening to fat people blame their genes for their obesity. Chances are they have not been able to fit in their jeans for years! People are fat because they eat too much. Period. Only about 1 percent of obesity is caused from thyroid problems or anything genetic. The primary reason people are fat is that they overeat and then they get little or no exercise. It is their own fault. Think about it: Did you ever eat anything by accident? It is not McDonald's fault you said, "Super-size that for me." None of the fast food places held a gun to your head and forced you to eat their food. You did it. It is your own fault and you are responsible for your fat belly—not them.

We have become so quick to blame others for our mistakes. We want to sue others for our mistakes. Look at these lawsuits I recently read about:

In Cleveland, Ohio, a man sued M&M/Mars and a local candy dealer for $500,000 to cover hospitalization and surgery bills. He bit through his lip when he chomped down on an M&M peanut that did not have a peanut in it.

In Boston, Massachusetts, a would-be lifeguard, who is totally deaf, sued the YMCA for $20 million for prejudicially and insensitively requiring its lifeguards to be able hear noises and distress signals.

In Raymondville, Texas, a man sued a dog owner for $25,000 after tripping over the dog in the man's kitchen, claiming the man neglected to warn him of the dog's propensity of lying in certain areas.

I know you have read or heard of other cases similar to these. While the examples are absurd, the point is simple: We have become a nation of blamers.

Stuff Is Going to Happen

We are *people*—stuff happens to *people*. When stuff happens to you it just proves you are alive, because as long as you live, stuff is going to happen. Stop thinking you are one of the special ones that nothing happens to. Those people do not exist, and if they did, who would really want to hang around them anyway? They would be so boring. What would they have to talk about? How perfect everything is in their lives? Would you just want to slap them?

The stuff that happens to you is what makes life interesting—both the good stuff *and* the bad stuff. It is called life. It is not perfect. It is just life. Deal with it. Put up with it. Enjoy it as best you can. But please, whatever you do, do not whine about it.

Someone sent me this from the Internet—it is one of those stupid things that get passed around with no one to give credit to, or I would happily do it. While most of the Internet "stories" are worthless, I liked this one:

IF . . .
If you can start the day without caffeine,
If you can always be cheerful, ignoring aches and pains,
If you can resist complaining and boring people with your troubles,
If you can eat the same food every day and be grateful for it,
If you can understand when your loved ones are too busy to give you any time,
If you can overlook it when those you love take it out on you when through no fault of yours, something goes wrong,
If you can take criticism and blame without resentment,

If you can resist treating a rich friend better than a poor friend,
If you can face the world without lies and deceit,
If you can conquer tension without medical help,
If you can relax without liquor,
If you can sleep without the aid of drugs,
If you can honestly say that deep in your heart that you have no preju-
    dice against creed, color, religion, gender preference, or politics,
Then you have reached the same level of development as your dog.

Life can be complicated and hard at times. Celebrate that. It is what makes us human. And interesting. And capable of dealing with all that happens.

"If you are going through hell, keep going."
—Winston Churchill

Few people will turn to themselves to take responsibility for their results until they have exhausted all opportunities to blame someone else.

"Whoa, Larry, cut me some slack!"

I will not! You *earn* slack. No one is going to cut you any slack except your momma, so stop asking others to cut you some slack. Why should they? Life does not issue Get Out of Jail Free cards for being stupid. Stop expecting the world to rescue you. The Lone Ranger is not coming. Clean up your own mess. Fix your own problem. Admit you are an idiot and commit to do better next time. Stop fixing the blame and start fixing the problem!

The Real Danger of Whining

Whining prolongs the problem. As long as you continue to whine about what is wrong with your life there will be no room for anything good to come into your life. That is just the way life works. You cannot focus on the solution when you are whining about the problem. You cannot do two things at once. Pick the one that moves you closer to where you want to be in life. Does whining bring you closer to success? Does whining bring you closer to a better relationship? Does whining really make you happy? Does it make you smile? Seriously, have you ever seen anyone smile and whine at the same time?

The answer obviously is that whining does not move you closer to where you want to be. Whining will only make your problem stick around longer. It will not make you smile. And trust me on this one, it will not endear you to others.

What moves you closer to where you want to be and what you want to have? A plan. When you have a plan for dealing with your situation, you are energized. You are happier. You are focused on the solution. That is when your life moves forward. And you cannot plan and whine at the same time.

Remember: You can only choose one thing to do, so what is it going to be? Are you going to whine and stay stuck? Or are you going to create a plan that moves you toward the life you want?

I Understand Problems

People have problems. People get laid off, they get fired, they get downsized, upsized and rightsized. I understand these things happen. And I understand they happen to really good people. That is the way life is—bad things do happen to really good people. I am not closing my eyes to these things. I am not saying you caused the economy to go south or your company to be sold. Those things are not your fault. But your reaction to those things happening *is* your fault.

Life does not just happen to you; you happen to life. So you got dealt a crummy hand. It happens. Pick up the cards, shuffle them, and deal yourself a new hand. You are in control. Do not wait. Do not whine. Good things do not interrupt you. You have to make them come. And that is what is up next: discovering how to get the life you always wanted.

> **If you don't have much going wrong in your life, then you don't have much going on in your life.**

CHAPTER 3

Get a Life!

"Life begins at the end of your comfort zone."
> —Neale Donald Walsch,
> *Conversations with God*, Book 3

So are you sick of living life in a "less than" way? Having less than you want? Less than you dreamed of? Less than you deserve? Are you finally ready to do something about it? Are you ready to change?

I doubt it.

"What? How can you be so cruel? How can you say you doubt that I am ready to change?"

Easy. I have heard it all before. You have probably said it all before as well.

I start every speech I give with these questions: "How many of you are ready to be more successful in the future than you ever were in the past? How many of you are ready to make more money in the future than you ever did in the past? How many of you are ready to have more fun in the future than you ever did in the past?" I ask them to respond by yelling out "You bet!" at the end of each question. Every-

one eagerly does. How many of those people do you think really become more successful, make more money, or have more fun? I doubt
if very many of them do. Your response might be that it is because I
did not give that great of a speech. That certainly could be. But I
think there is much more to it than that.

Ready, Willing, and Able

Remember the old saying "Ready—Willing—Able"? We have heard
that most of our lives. It is one of the most recognizable clichés.

READY

Here is how I look at that statement: Everyone is ready. Or at least
they think they are, or say they are. That is why they all yell "You bet!"
at the questions I ask in my speeches. And I actually think when people say they are ready, they are. I honestly have never met anyone
who was not ready for more.

ABLE

Skip to the third item on the list: able. How many are able? Everyone.
Seriously. No matter what you face; whether it is a mental, financial,
or physical liability, you are still able to do more. Even if it is just a little bit more. The great news is that when you do a little more, your results can increase by a lot more.

So, if everyone really is *ready* to do better and to have more, and
everyone really is *able* to do more and become more, then what is
the problem?

WILLING

The answer to that question lies in the second word of the cliché: willing. Is everyone *willing* to become more or to do more in order to have what they want in life? The answer is a screaming NO! And that is the problem. People are not willing to put in the hours or expend the effort to change. The world really is not made up of the "have's" and the "have-not's." It is made up of the "will's" and the "will-not's."

Again, the question is never, "*Can* someone do better?" Of course they can. And it is never, "Are they *able* to do better?" Of course they are able. The question is always, "*Will* they do better?" Sorry, but most just will not. Not because they cannot and not because they are not able, but simply because they are not willing.

See how simple it is? You have probably been asking yourself for a good long time why your life is not better. Now you have the answer. The answer is that you are not willing to do what it takes for your life to be better.

"That doesn't sound very fair."

Of course it does. It is perfectly fair. Your life is the way it is because you have not been willing to do what it takes to make it different. Period. Case closed.

And sadly, it is not that you have not wanted it to be better. Want has little to do with it. You can desperately want success and never achieve it. You can want to be rich and never make any money. You can want to lose weight and only get fatter. Want only matters if you want enough to be willing to do whatever it takes to achieve the desired result.

Three More Reasons People Are Not Successful

I have already told you one of the reasons you are not successful: You have not been willing to do what it takes. But since I know people do not like just one reason, I am going to give you three more—three I know you will not like at all!

1. You are stupid.
2. You are lazy.
3. You do not give a damn.

Three Main Reasons People Are Not Successful:

They are stupid.

They are lazy.

They don't give a damn.

Ouch! Still recoiling a bit from that? A little too harsh for you? Too bad. It is still true, and remember: the truth hurts!

The common word in each of these reasons is *you*. You are the reason your life sucks. In other words, if your life sucks it is because you suck. It is not because conditions suck. It is you.

We are all given the same list of things in life to deal with:

▌ The economy.
▌ Taxes.
▌ Insurance.
▌ Aging.
▌ Stupid people we have to work with.
▌ Kids that drive us crazy.
▌ Bills.

▮ Crazy customers.
▮ Not enough time.
▮ Not enough money.

Does this list look familiar to you? It should because all of us have basically similar lists. While we all have a list that looks much the same, some people take the list and get rich while other people take the list and go broke. You know what? It is not the list's fault. It is your fault.

You want a list of reasons you are not doing well? Here's one: You.

> ## If your life sucks, it is because you suck.

Stop making worthless, flimsy excuses and face the music: you are either stupid, lazy, or you do not give a damn.

These are excuses. These are not reasons. There is a big difference. Reasons are real. Excuses are not real. Yes, they exist, but they are not real in the sense that they are keeping you from doing well. They are only excuses that give you a way to keep from accepting responsibility. Excuses allow you to point the finger of blame away from yourself. Reasons force you to point the finger of blame in the direction it should be pointed—in your own face.

I will listen to a reason. I will even try to understand it. I may even do my best to tolerate it. And I will give you a little while to deal with and overcome it. But excuses? Sorry, no slack when it comes to excuses.

Let me make it clear here that I do understand adverse conditions. All of us go through tough times. However, we cannot use tough times as an excuse forever. Enough of that—I already beat you up about that in Chapter 2. I want to more closely examine the three reasons people are not as successful as they want to be.

YOU ARE STUPID

Now that I have said it, I want you to know I have a hard time buying this one. None of us knows everything, even though I often get accused of thinking I do. And all of us can certainly afford to know more than we already do. In fact, you should be reading and listening and learning more every day. Information has never been more abundant or more easily accessible. Libraries are plentiful; bookstores are on almost every corner and most even serve good coffee; the Internet is available to most and has lots of interesting things to learn (in fact, you can find things on the Internet you do not even want to know). So if you are interested in finding information, there is plenty of it around.

Lack of information, though, is not the problem. And stupidity is not really the problem. How many people are really stupid? (Please do not raise your hand here!) I do not believe there are that many stupid people. People know enough just the way they are to be successful. Really. There is not a person who does not know enough to be successful at something. You may not know enough to be successful at anything or at everything—but you know enough to be successful at something.

The problem is not that you do not know. The problem is that you do not do what you already know. That is the crux of the matter. You know enough, but you are not doing much with it. In other words, you are not really stupid at all. You are lazy.

YOU ARE LAZY

Here is another popular cliché: Knowledge is power. You have heard this your whole life. Yet this cliché is a lie. In fact, I think this is one of the most unfortunate lies ever perpetuated on society. Knowledge is not power. It is the implementation of knowledge that is power.

**Knowledge is not power.
It is the implementation of knowledge that is power.**

It is not what you know that matters, it is what you do with what you know that matters. Knowledge alone will not fix anything. It takes effort. It does not always take a lot of effort—but it takes at least some effort.

The good news is that some effort is just about all it takes to do well these days. There are many ways to make a living. You can make a living doing about anything. In fact, I am going to go out on a limb here and say that no one has to be without a job if they really want one.

I know a person who picks up dog poop for a living. Really. In fact, she used to pick up my dog's poop. She would show up once a week, spend about five minutes scooping doggie poop and move on to the next house and the next pile of poop. Her slogan: "We're #1 in #2."

Is this a crummy way to make a living? Maybe for you. But this woman loves her job. She drives a brand new truck, spends her time in the outdoors, which she loves, and gets to say howdy to lots of wonderful dogs, which she also loves.

One day a young man about 20 years old rang my doorbell. He had a bucket that contained a couple of cans of spray paint and some number stencils. He wanted to spray my house numbers on my curb as mine had faded over the years. Four numbers with a background — all for only five bucks. Five bucks? I said sure and handed over the five bucks. Two minutes later he had finished. He then walked next door and rang my neighbor's doorbell and the process started all over again. I talked to him while he did my neighbor's curb. He explained that he attended college at the University of Oklahoma and had been painting house numbers on curbs for the past two summers. In about 75 days he makes enough money to pay his tuition and room and board for the whole year — at five bucks a whack.

The point here is that there are plenty of ways to make a living. It just takes a willingness to get off your lazy butt and do something. It seems most people would rather be broke and lazy than work a little and have a pocket full of money. They complain being broke is so terrible and in their mind they are saying, "but at least I won't have to break a sweat."

It takes very little effort to get a job these days. Companies will hire you no matter how little you know. All they really want is for you to show up every day. (Standards are pretty low these days it seems.) Maybe you will not be getting hired for the job of your dreams, but at least you will be doing something and earning a paycheck. You will have your dignity and some self-respect. Many companies will hire you with no training and no experience and no skills and then train you. Good news! You can be stupid and still get hired.

Plus, there are plenty of educational programs that are either free or cost very little to attend that will give you specialized skills so you can land a really good paying job. There are books that will teach you everything there is to know about a given subject. It is not for lack of information that you are not doing well — it is for lack of effort. It does not take a lot of effort to read a book, does it? In fact, you can sit on your lazy butt and do that. But will you? I hope so, but the reality of the situation is that most will not. So will you? Sadly the odds are not in your favor. Why not?

YOU DO NOT GIVE A DAMN

This is the really ugly reason. This is the one that will paralyze you and keep you broke and unhappy.

I will cut you a little slack if you are truly stupid—at least for a while. You do not get any slack if you are lazy. But if you do not care enough to be more and do better, I will not be able to stand being in your presence.

Not giving a damn, or not caring, is the ultimate insult to yourself and to your family. To know how to be successful and not care enough to do it is truly a pitiful thing.

How can you look your family in the eye and admit to them you are able to provide a better life for them but will not because you do not love them enough to read a book, take a class, get up a little earlier, turn off the TV a little quicker, or work a little harder or longer?

"Not fair!" you say. Oh sure it is. If you are mentally and physically able to be better than you are, and to do better than you do, and you do not do it—the only reason I can come up with is that you do not care enough about yourself and your family to do so. Sorry, but that makes me sick.

Let us cut to the chase here. Stop right now and admit you could do more than you are doing. And I do not really care how much you are doing—you could do a little more. Right?

And because you bought this book, you have probably decided you are ready to do more. And maybe you just need a guide to show you the way. Okay, then let us get started.

Time to Get Started

Hopefully you are ready. By this time you have stopped your whining, put away all of your excuses, and are ready to create the life of your dreams. But before you do that you need to spend a little time actually designing that life. You cannot just run after what you want until you really know exactly what you want.

"But I do know what I want. I want more!"

Okay, here is a dollar. Now you have more. If I gave you a dollar you would have more, right? But that is not what you had in mind, is it? I know it is not. But it is still what you said. You have to be specific.

In the next few pages I am going to help you specifically design the life you want and teach you how to create it.

Get ready—this is going to be fun!

CHAPTER 4

How to Live
by Design,
Not by Default

"We are all self-made. But only the successful will admit it."
—Anonymous

You have created everything that has happened in your life: both the good and the bad. I had a complete business failure and both a business and personal bankruptcy that were my own fault. I created those things. I created every single problem I ever had. I also created my business success and the happiness I am experiencing now. You created your situation, too. It was easy. All you and I did was think, speak, and do.

What you think about, talk about, and do something about is what comes about. That is how you created your messes and your successes. That is how I did it too.

**What you think about,
talk about, and do something about
is what comes about.**

It is your thoughts, words, and actions that will either move you closer to where you want to be or further away from where you want to be. Those three things are the keys to creating the life you want and have been the keys to the life you are currently living.

You see, you never have a money problem, a relationship problem, a business problem, or a health problem. You only have a problem with how you think, what you say, and your actions. And when you straighten out your thoughts, words and actions, everything will be fine.

Thoughts are creative. Words are creative. Actions are creative. These are the three creative forces of the Universe. Master these and the world belongs to you.

Change Your Thoughts

"All that we are arises with our thoughts."

—Buddha

Limited thinking produces limited results. Results are the way you live, what you are experiencing, and the stuff you have.

Limited thinking comes from a limited view of who you are. When you expand your vision of who you are then you will be able to think in bigger ways.

When you are able to think differently of yourself and your abilities to accomplish your desires, you will think differently about the rest of the world as well. Then you will express yourself differently (your words), and you will act differently, too.

"The secret of living a life of excellence is merely a matter of thinking thoughts of excellence."

—Charles Swindoll

Think of what the highest vision of yourself would be. When picturing your highest vision of yourself stop and ask, "Is this thought in alignment with my highest vision of myself?" If not, then change the thought.

> "Daily we must train our thoughts to see only what we wish to experience; and since we are growing into what we are mentally dwelling upon, we should put all small and insignificant thoughts and ideals out of our thinking and see things in a larger way."
>
> —Ernest Holmes

Tag Yourself with Words

> "For by your words you will be justified, and by your words you will be condemned."
>
> —Matthew 12:37 KJV

Tag yourself a winner. Several years ago I got a personalized license plate for my car that said, "WINNER." I had no idea at the time the kind of impact that tag would have on my life. I found out that with a tag on your car that says WINNER, you could no longer do the things you have been used to doing. You cannot pull out in front of people and cut them off (not that I would ever do that!). And why not? Would a WINNER do that? No, only a loser would do that. Would a WINNER honk at people who cut them off, or who pull away too slowly from a red light? No, a WINNER would never do that, only a loser would. Would a WINNER drive a dirty car? Sorry, only a loser would drive a dirty car. I had tagged myself a WINNER and suddenly my actions had to change in order to back up what I was saying about myself. I became more of a winner in life simply because I had pro-claimed to all who saw me that I was a winner.

Call yourself something and you will become that something. Call yourself a winner and you become more of a winner. Call your-self broke, stupid, unable—live a life full of can'ts, won'ts, should have's, would have's, I wish I had's and if only's, and see what you be-come. I bet you will not be happy with the results.

Change Your Words

Think again of what your highest vision of yourself would be. When picturing your highest vision of yourself stop and ask, "Are the words I use in alignment with my highest vision of myself?" If not, then change the way you are talking.

Saying things like, "I have never been able to do that well" will only perpetuate the fact you will not ever be able to it well. Saying "I'm not good at math" does not make you better at math. Saying "Food always goes straight to my thighs" means you are going to have fat thighs as a result of your eating. "I always get a cold this time of year" is the surest way I know of to catch a cold.

What you say programs what happens. Your words attract to you either the life you want, or the life you do not want.

When I was in the telecommunications business, it got to the point I hated going to work. I had the "Sunday Night Blues." Every Sunday night I would just get a bad feeling knowing the next morn-ing I had to get up and go to an office and do something I did not like doing any longer. One day I told my wife, "I'd give anything to not have to do this any more." The Universe heard me and started to attract that result into my life. The problem was that the Universe did not hear me very clearly. It thought I had said that I would give *everything* not to have to do this anymore. So that is what ended up happening to me. I ended up giving everything I had, and then no longer had to go to work there any longer. I lost it all—my job, my company, my money, my cars, everything. Be careful what you say. It happens.

Instead of saying what you do not want to happen, begin today proclaiming what you do want to happen. Start with the affirmation I am giving you here. Then go on to create your own personalized versions.

THIS DAY

This day, I thankfully accept all of the good things that are coming my way. This day is full of excitement, love, energy, health, and prosperity. This day, people are calling on me to be of service to them and I respond by giving my very best. This day, I think and practice health in my life, refusing to accept anything less than perfect health. This day, I accept the abundance and prosperity that is mine and willingly share it with others. This day, I focus on the moment and give no thought to the past or to the future. This day, I spend in total enjoyment of what I do. This day, I fill with loving thoughts and actions toward all other people and myself. This day, I spend in grateful appreciation of all that is mine. This day, this hour, this minute, this moment is all that I have and I choose to use it in celebration!

I have personally used this affirmation for many years. I read it to myself daily. When my mind forgets to focus on the right things and doubts creep in, I read it several times a day. If this affirmation does not seem to fit your style, then write your own. Say the things you need to hear to help create the life you want.

Affirmations are powerful. However, do not think that affirmations alone are going to change things for you. Just saying something will not change your results. Affirmation without implementation is self-delusion. You cannot skip the "do" side of the equation.

Change Your Actions

Your actions are the result of your thoughts, and beliefs. If you act in a way that produces negative results, it is because you harbor thoughts and beliefs that support that action.

Think of what your highest vision of yourself would be. When picturing your highest vision of yourself stop and ask, "Is this action in alignment with my highest vision of myself?" In other words, is this the best I see for myself or can I see something better? Keep asking until you see the very best thing for yourself and then act according to that picture of yourself.

"But you don't understand, that's just how I do things. I've always done things that way."

Exactly. And that is why you have what you have. You have what you have because you have always done things the way you do them. If you want something different, you have to change the way you do things. So change!

Everyone always wants to know how to change, and I am about to tell you. And I promise you will not like the answer. You just change. See? I told you that you would not like it. You wanted a complicated answer. A long, drawn out process with steps you could tick off as you accomplished them. Sorry. It is not like that. To change, you just change.

Remember how you did things yesterday? Do not do them that way today. Do not think the way you did. Do not talk the way you did. Do not act the way you did.

> "As long as you keep on doing what you've been doing then you are going to keep on getting what you've been getting. If you don't like what you've been getting then you've got to change what you've been doing."
>
> —Zig Ziglar

Got it yet? It is not as hard as you might think. Some say start small and build up, and change the little things first. Wrong! Change the way you think, the way you talk, the people you hang around with, the places you go, the things you read, the food you eat, the television you watch. Change all of it. If I were broke, unhappy, and unsuccessful, I would be willing to change the way I brush my teeth—if I thought it might make a difference. Remember that the stuff you do now has determined the results you have now. If you do not like those results, then change what you are doing right now.

> **"If you want something you have never had, you have to do something you have never done."**
>
> —Mike Murdock

Stop Trying

I have probably just about convinced you to get started. You are about to say, "Okay, Larry, I'll try." Then forget it. Do not even start if you are only going to try. I hate the word *try*. Yoda, the little green Jedi philosopher from *Star Wars*, was right when he said, "There is no try. There is only do or do not do."

When someone tells you they will try to come to your party, do you really expect them to show up? I doubt that you do. When you tell someone you are going to try to go to their party, do you really plan on going? I do not think so.

Try is a word you use when you do not have the cajones to tell the truth. We should all just be honest. You ask me, "Are you going to come to my party?" I answer with, "No. I don't want to come to your party. I would rather gouge out my eye with a carrot stick than come to your stupid, boring, lame party!" That is honesty!

But none of us would ever do that would we? Of course not. It is just easier to say, "I will try." Mostly try is an excuse to yourself. It gives you a way out. "Yes I will do it" is a commitment. You can be held to a commitment. You cannot really hold someone to a try because when they do not do it, they can always offer you their patented cop-out of, "Oh well, I tried."

My advice is to stop trying and stop saying you will try. Instead just do it or do not do it. How do you try anyway? Stop right now and try to pick up a pencil or pen or whatever is lying next to you. Really, just try to do it. You cannot. There is no way to try to pick something up. You either pick it up or you do not pick it up. Period. There is no in-between. Try is an excuse not to do. Give it up. By the way, I am having a party soon. Please try to come!

Nothing Is Neutral

Everything you think, everything you say, and everything you do matters. It all moves you one direction or the other. Every little "I can't do this" moves you further away from your goal. Every conversation, as meaningless as it may seem to you, means a lot when it comes to achieving what you want.

"So when I am talking to my friends or my co-workers in the hall, you are saying that idle chit-chat has an impact on me getting rich, or healthy, or successful or happy?"

Exactly. Every word matters. If your conversations are full of complaining or putting people down, and you focus on what you lack, then those conversations are killing your chances for success.

The same applies to every action you take. Sitting through one more television show instead of playing with your kids or having a conversation with your spouse or partner may not seem like a big deal at the time—but it matters.

Sleeping another thirty minutes instead of getting up and exercising matters. Not calling your customer back at the agreed time matters. Showing up fifteen minutes late matters.

"Oh come on! This is little stuff. You can't be serious. This stuff doesn't matter—I have been doing stuff just like this for years and nothing bad has happened."

Has anything amazing happened? When you stop letting things slide and start taking advantage of every moment then amazing things happen. The little stuff matters the most. Everyone gets the big stuff. Very few take care of the little stuff. That is why very few end up rich, successful, happy, and healthy, with great relationships. They take care of the big things and let the little things slide. That is a surefire way to live a life of mediocrity. Not much bad—but not much amazing either.

TATTOOED FOR LIFE

My wife and I were sitting in a bar one evening having a cocktail when a young woman (about 30, but still a young woman at this point in my life) struck up a conversation with us. She said she bet I rode a motorcycle. I asked her how she could tell and she said I just had the look: shaved head, goatee, boots, and sunglasses. She then added that she bet I had some tattoos as well. I confirmed that I indeed have several.

She proudly told us she also had one and proceeded to show us her tattoo, which was a broken heart. She was so proud of it. I asked her why she would tattoo a broken heart on her hip. She said she just thought it was pretty. I asked her why she would want to proclaim to the world and to every man she met and even to herself that she had a broken heart? I went on to ask her how her love life was going. She said it sucked; she could not keep a boyfriend, and every man in her life treated her horribly.

I asked her when that trend started. She replied that it had all started about five years earlier. I then asked how long she'd had the tattoo of the broken heart, and she said about five years. I asked if she could see any correlation between the two events. A light came on in her eyes and she said, "You don't think the tattoo is causing my love life to be bad, do you?" My wife, Rose Mary, and I both assured her that indeed we did. She asked what she should do and we told her she should get that tattoo filled in as soon as possible. That way she would be proclaiming to the world and to every man she dated—and to her-self—that her heart was whole and full. She said thanks, gave us both a hug, and left immediately to go to the tattoo parlor.

The lesson? Be careful what you proclaim to the world to be true about yourself whether it be through your words, your actions, or your tattoo. Even the little things can have a big impact.

Go for the amazing life. Take care of the little stuff—do the stuff most will never do. Know that every little thing you think, say, and do has a major impact on the outcome of your life.

Design Your Life

You do not get what you want until you know what you want. Other-wise you get what is left over. I hate leftovers. I want to create some-thing new and perfect just for me.

Following is a questionnaire that will help you determine exactly what you want out of life. Take the time right now to fill it out. Do not rush. Take your time and give it some thought. We are not in any hurry here. Be very specific in your answers—remember this is your life you are creating.

What would I like to accomplish before I die?

What do I want to own that I do not currently own?

What kind of car do I really want to drive?

What kind of house do I want to live in?

At which stores do I really want to shop?

What kind of clothes would I like to wear?

What kind of jewelry would I like to wear?

Which restaurants do I want to go to?

Where would I like to travel?

How would I like to spend my recreational time?

Which people would I like to spend more time with?

What would I really like to do if time and money were not issues?

How much would I like to weigh?

How much money would I like to earn each year?

How much money would I like to have saved/invested?

How much money would I like to give away each year?

What kind of relationship do I want with my spouse/significant other/partner/lover/special friend?
. . . with my children?
. . . with my family?
. . . with my co-workers?
. . . with my friends?
. . . with God?

Summarize your perfect life in the next few lines:

_____

_____

_____

_____

How did you do? Does your new life look significantly different than your current life? I bet it does. Now it is time for some honesty. It is time to look at what you are currently doing to make this life happen. Here is another list for you to work on. It is a list of things you are actually doing to make the life you want to come about. If you do not know where to start, you can answer number one with "I am reading this book and filling out these forms." There. You have the first one. Now keep going.

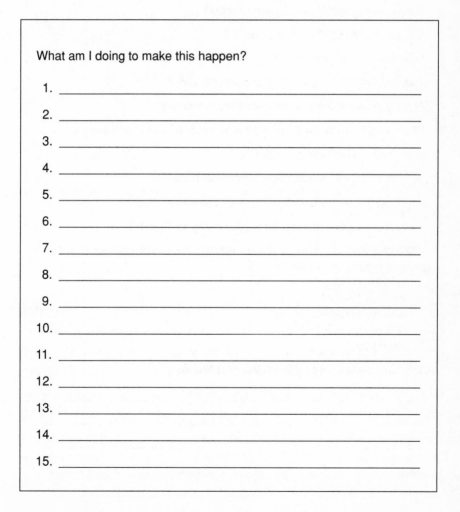

What am I doing to make this happen?

1. _____
2. _____
3. _____
4. _____
5. _____
6. _____
7. _____
8. _____
9. _____
10. _____
11. _____
12. _____
13. _____
14. _____
15. _____

Okay that is what you *say* you are doing. And I will bet you the price of this book you did not get to 15. Very few people are actually doing even 15 things to create the life they want to live. And I even gave you the first one! Now let me give you another shot at telling yourself the truth.

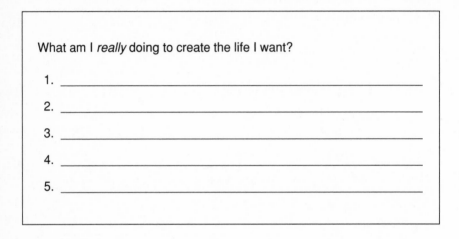

What am I *really* doing to create the life I want?

1. _____

2. _____

3. _____

4. _____

5. _____

There you go. Did you do better this time? Did you come up with five things you are *really* doing? I hope so. Soon you will be able to fill the first list too. As you start creating the life you want with just a few action steps, you will find that things get easier for you. You will start to focus more and more on creating the life you want until you reach the point where you are obsessed with living the life most only dream of. You will actually find yourself becoming the list you made. You will look in the mirror and see yourself in the clothes you want to wear, with the jewelry you want to wear, weighing what you want to weigh. You will go to your garage and get in the car you want to drive and go to the restaurant where you really want to go. You will enjoy your relationships and have plenty of time to relax and enjoy your life. In other words, you will be creating the life you want.

A word of caution: The life you want comes at a price. Everything comes at a price. Nothing is free. No matter what it is in life you choose, there will be a price tag attached.

Want to be fit, trim, and healthy? The price tag is decreased calories and increased exercise.

Want to be rich? You either have to work harder, longer, or smarter—probably all three. There will not be as much time for television. There will not be as much time for golf. Wealth has its price.

Want to be successful? The price tag is pretty expensive, as you are about to find out.

Want to be happy? Then you have to give up everything that makes you unhappy.

And what if you do not want anything? That comes at a price, too. The price is usually poverty, sickness, boredom, apathy, mediocrity, bad relationships, and on and on and on.

The reality of life is that you will pay a price, one way or the other. One price gives you exactly what you want. The other gives you exactly what you do not want. Either way, you have paid the price.

The good news is that the life you want comes cheaper than the life you do not want. The life you do not want makes you miserable, unhealthy, and broke. To me, that is too big a price to pay. It is cheaper to be happy, healthy, and rich. However, only you can choose what to pay.

CHAPTER 5

Slaughtering the Sacred Self-Help Cows

You have just spent some time thinking about the life you want. Hopefully you now have a picture of the kind of life you want to lead. You even wrote it down—probably for the very first time in your life. You say you are willing to pay the price. Congratulate yourself! You are now further along than almost any other person on the planet. Very few people have ever made it as far as you just have.

So let us get real about making the life you have designed really happen for you. Let us look at all the areas of life each of us deals with and discover how to move through them and past them to actually get the life you want.

This is where you probably think I am going to address all of the typical self-help stuff like setting and achieving goals, being positive, and that sort of motivational mumbo-jumbo. No. I am going to give you stuff that is much different than what you have come across before. In fact, I am going to attack most of what you have heard and read and learned.

Some will not like my approach here, but as you have probably figured out by now . . . I do not care.

And some will think I am not telling the truth because it is so contrary to what we have been bombarded with for so long, but that does not make it untrue. It just makes it unconventional, which, in my opinion, makes it refreshing and worth looking at.

"All great truth begins as blasphemy."

—George Bernard Shaw

Attitude and Motivation

Let me begin with two things I am absolutely positive of: attitude is not everything and motivation does not work.

"What? How can you say that? You lie! You are a bad man! I buy books by motivational speakers all the time! I go to hear motivational speakers whenever I get a chance. I listen to motivational tapes and am the biggest and best customer of Nightingale-Conant and Career-Track. So what do you mean attitude isn't everything and motivation doesn't work?"

Well, let me prove it to you. If you are the kind of person you say you are, listening to motivational speakers and reading motivational self-help books, then answer these questions: How is your life? Are you rich, happy, healthy, and successful? No? Well there you go, that stuff doesn't really work, does it? (By the way, if you really are rich, happy, healthy, and successful, then congratulations. But I promise you motivation is not what got you there.)

Don't you just hate that? You are caught. Don't feel bad. I used to be just like you. I have read literally thousands of motivational, self-help books. I have also listened to at least that many motivational, self-help tapes. I have been to lots of meetings and heard the high-powered, high-priced motivational gurus (some of whom are now my good friends) say all those things about feeling good about yourself and how you have to be positive every waking moment. I have listened to them tell the masses to just have a good attitude and anything will be possible. I would sit on the edge of my seat and eat it up until I would nearly swoon with the idea that if only I had the right attitude, my life would be okay.

Listen, I have had a good, positive attitude all my life and I have had more crap happen to me than you can imagine! I had a great attitude and went bankrupt. I had a great attitude the whole time I had problems in my business, my marriage, with my money, and my health. That wonderful, positive attitude of mine did not keep one thing from happening to me.

So regardless of what any of the books, tapes, and speakers say, attitude is not everything. I know that is a lot to swallow since it flies in the face of what everyone else says and everything you have ever heard. Like you, I have seen books out there telling you attitude is everything. You can find coasters and T-shirts and even buy a cute little rock to use as a paperweight that says, "Attitude is Everything." You can even get little coins to carry in your pocket to remind you of the same sentiment. You can buy posters to line your walls. It makes the suckers feel better and lines the pockets of the manufacturers. And it is still a lie because attitude is not everything!

ATTITUDE IS IMPORTANT

Attitude is important; I will give you that. But it will not keep anything from happening to you. It will help you deal with what happens to you, but it will not keep anything from happening to you. So while it is important, it certainly is not everything. Attitude is only one thing.

What people sometimes think is if they get their attitude right then they will have no problems, they will have nothing bad happen to them, and they will not even have to work—simply because their attitude is so good.

Attitude alone will not change things. Effort changes things. Thoughts change things. Words change things. Again, remember this: It is what you think about, talk about, and do something about that comes about. That is what changes things: the combination of those three things. It is not what you have a positive attitude about!

It takes more than being positive, because you can be positively lazy. You can be positively wrong. You can be positively stupid.

HAVE A NEGATIVE ATTITUDE SOMETIMES

Sometimes I have a crappy attitude. I mean it is totally negative. How about you?

You will not often hear a self-help guy admit to having a bad attitude. But I am not your typical self-help guy. I gladly admit I am very negative sometimes. I have days where I am anything but positive. I need days like that. You need those days, too.

"Now Larry, that doesn't make any sense. Why would I need to be negative? Why would you need a negative attitude?"

Being negative serves me well. I think it will serve you well, too. Some days you need to get ticked off at yourself—mad at the way things are going and mad at yourself for being the kind of person you are. Mad at the way you are raising your kids—mad at the way you are behaving with your spouse—mad at the way you are running your business. Anger and a bad attitude are sometimes great motivators. Sometimes you have to get upset in order to change things.

In order to make positive changes *in* your life, you first have to get negative *about* your life.

It is not about being positive or negative; it is about what works and what does not work. It is about what moves you from where you are to someplace else. It is about what makes things better for you.

It is like those people who ask that old, stupid question: Is the glass half empty or half full? My answer? Who the hell cares?

What difference does it make if the glass is half full or half empty? Here is the real issue. Does it quench your thirst? That is what matters. Attitude alone will not quench your thirst. It will not move you from where you are to someplace else. That is why I am not a motivational speaker. Instead I call myself The World's Only Irritational Speaker™. I am just not sure I can motivate you to move from where you are to someplace else. However, I am very confident that I can make you so irritated with where you are that you will do anything you can to be someplace else.

**In order to make positive changes *in* your life,
you first have to get negative *about* your life.**

COMBINE ATTITUDE WITH WORK

Work: a dirty word. You are paid for effort—the effort to serve others well. Service is rewarded. Always. It is a Universal Law. Earl Nightingale said, "Your rewards in life are in direct proportion to your service." A lofty idea that sounds so sweet to say. However, service comes disguised as work. Effective service to others usually requires a little sweat. You should perform your work with a good attitude. But even work performed with a bad attitude gets rewarded. Attitude does not get you paid; work gets you paid. Work performed with a good attitude will get you paid better and will make the work go faster and will definitely be more fun, but the key ingredient to doing well is still the work, the effort, and the service!

You are paid for:

> . . . the effort to help others.
> . . . the effort to serve others.
> . . . the effort to love others.
> . . . the effort to bring happiness to others.
> . . . the effort to make others' lives more secure.
> . . . the effort to make others' lives easier.

The effort you put forth in your life and your business must address this list. Sound new-agey, metaphysical, philosophical, and spiritual? It is!

Do not panic; what you are doing already fits the list. Every business in some way provides a product or service that fits the list. If it did not, it would cease to exist. The key is to understand the list and to get better at it. Businesses that understand it and practice it, thrive. Those that do not, eventually go belly up.

People who understand that their purpose is service to others live lives of abundance. Those who do not just live their lives.

Serve Others Well

Service must be the ultimate motive of your life. Your work is the way you perform the service. Success, happiness, and prosperity come from having served well.

You have been to the seminars and I am sure you have heard this: "We are not human doings; we are human beings."

I bet you have heard the motivational hot shots say that, right? Why do you think they say it? It sells, that's why. I have even said it myself. I am not proud of it, but I have. Forgive me, but in the past even I sold out a few times.

The idea behind that statement is that people should focus more on who they are rather than what they do. We have become a nation so caught up in doing that we have forgotten the importance of being. Well, it sounds good but it is not true. The truth is that we are not a nation of doers; we are a nation of watchers. We sit on our big, fat butts and watch television. We have become a nation of voyeurs. We like to watch people date on television instead of having a real date ourselves. We watch someone else cook a meal while we eat fast food. We enjoy watching other people play sports, decorate their homes, get makeovers, organize their garage, and have sex. All while we sit on our butts. We would rather watch than do. Fewer risks. Less effort. We like to say we are doers, but face it, the few do and the many watch. And much of what the many do is gripe and complain about the few who do, because it should have been done differently. It makes me sick! Stop watching so much and start doing something!

We like to say that we are "human beings and not human doings." It gets us off the hook for not doing anything. It tells us to forget the doing and focus on the being. I love the idea we should focus on being better people. Of course we should. We should all become as good as we can. We should become as spiritual as we can, as smart as we can, as loving as we can, as healthy as we can, as successful as we can, as rich as we can, and on and on. But will we? Most never will. Why? It takes effort. In order to be more you have to do something.

It takes effort to be spiritual, smart, loving, healthy, successful, rich. That is why so few achieve those things. They will not put in the effort. They want to think themselves into a better life. Or contemplate their way to a better life. It will not work. You can sit under a tree and contemplate your navel until the end of eternity and until you get up, dust off your butt, and go do something, very little is going to change.

I am not playing down the importance of meditation, quiet time, prayer, introspection, or whatever it is you want to call it or however you want to practice it. I do it myself. It is a wonderful thing. However, the purpose of those acts is to bring about clarity of purpose; to make clearer what we are destined to do once we stand back up; to bring into focus our way of serving others through our efforts.

If You Want to Have a Better Life . . . Do Something!

I believe we have forgotten our English lessons. Actually that is pretty obvious; just listen to the conversations going on around you. It sounds like most people never even had an English lesson, much less remember their lessons. Them people ain't got no idea how to talk good irregardless of what they been learnt.

So, look again at an old English lesson. Remember state-of-being verbs? The state-of-being verbs are: is, am, are, was, and were. They reflect our "state of being." They do not reflect any state of action. That is the stuff you were taught in elementary school. However, we sell these verbs just a bit short because they actually do reflect action. Let me explain:

If you are, you must do.
Because anything that is, does.
So if you do not, then you are not.

Are you? Of course you are. And since you are, you must do. I am not implying you are not doing something. You are doing something. You are watching television, eating too much, griping . . . but why am I telling you? Look at your day and make your own list!

So it is not that you are not doing; you *are* doing. You are just not doing anything productive. You are not serving anyone. You are not helping anyone. You are not really doing anything except sitting on your butt and watching the world go by: the big, cruel world that treats you so badly and keeps you broke and unhappy. Due to your lack of doing the right things, you are not really successful. You are not rich. You are not happy. Fix it!

YOU MUST DO THE RIGHT THINGS

What are the right things? I do not need to tell you. You know what they are. You know exactly what you need to do to change your life completely for the better. The problem is never that we do not know; it is always that we do not do what we already know. So I am not going to insult you by making you a cute little list that reads, "Just Do This Stuff" and you will be okay.

Am I totally against motivation and self-help? Not at all. I make my living in that industry. In fact, this is a self-help book.

But look at those two concepts: motivation and self-help. People think of those as separate things. The key is to put those two concepts together. The only way to become motivated is to help yourself. It is up to you: not a book, a tape, or a speech. And it is not up to any speaker, teacher, or preacher either. None of those can really motivate you, so do not look to them. Do not count on them. Does that sound strange to hear from a guy who has written over a dozen self-help books, has recorded many audio and video series, and who makes his living speaking? It may sound strange, but the truth often does. I do not believe any book or tape or speech can really motivate you. Those things can only help you to motivate yourself. You will only change when you are ready to change, want to change, and believe that you can. A book, a tape, or a speech only serves you well when it makes you believe that you can. And most motivational tools can't do that. Instead, they make you feel good about who you are *already*. Feeling good about yourself will not move you from where you are to where you want to be.

That is why I say motivation does not work. If it did, then motivational speakers would run the world and they would be zillionaires. Trust me, they do not run the world and they are not zillionaires. I do not underestimate the value of what some motivational speakers say; I owe a lot to many of them. But I do not owe any of them for teaching me that feeling good about who I am will make a difference. I do, however, owe a great deal to those who reminded me instead to feel good about what I can do.

Feeling Good about Yourself Versus Believing in Yourself

This is what you need to understand: Motivation that makes you feel good about yourself will not change your life. Knowing you can do whatever you want to do will change your life. You have to move from feeling good about yourself to believing in your abilities. There is a major difference between the two concepts. Who cares if you feel good about yourself? Instead, believe in your abilities. That belief will propel you to amazing heights. You will believe you have the abilities to accomplish amazing things. And you do!

Most speakers and most books and tapes teach the concept backwards. Many of us have said that in order to have, you must do. And in order to do, you must be. In other words, if I feel good about whom I am, then I will be able to do anything.

Heard that before? Well, that might work; in a fairytale world that might work. Our society will not help you feel good about who you are. You are constantly reminded you are just not good enough. You know what? You are never going to feel good enough about yourself to do whatever you want to do. But should that stop you? Hell, no. It is not about feeling. You are never going to feel you have enough going for you to accomplish anything you want to accomplish. Does it mean that you cannot accomplish what you want to accomplish? Absolutely not. You can do just about anything you want to do. But you will not do it by feeling good about yourself. In this case, and maybe only in this case, feeling takes a back seat. It takes a back seat to fact. The feeling forced down our throats by the rest of the world and even by ourselves is that we cannot do what we want. The fact is, you can. So just do it. That is the only way to get it done. You will only do it by doing it. You just have to start. You have to do it and do it and do it. You have to do it badly to begin with. You have to keep doing it until you instill in yourself the courage to do a little more. That is how things get done: by doing something, whether you feel good about yourself or not. And things get done when you take action, whether you have a good attitude about it or a bad attitude. So do something. Anything. Even if you do the wrong thing, you will find out quicker than by not doing anything at all. So do it. Get started. Now.

SELF-IMAGE IS NOT THE KEY

Motivational speakers will tell you the key is self-image. The key is not self-image. Self-image is based on the words "I am." How I feel about myself based on who I am. Well, face it; you are not who you want to be. Whaaaa! Too bad. Why not just sit in the corner and whine about it? Maybe Oprah or Jerry or Montel will have you on their show so you can get the whole world to feel sorry for you. That way you can whine about it instead of taking responsibility for it. Surely that will help.

How you feel about who you are is just not that important. How you feel about what you "can do" is what is important. The key is self-*can*-age. I made that word up. My word is based on how you feel about yourself based on what you can do. And you can do just about anything you commit yourself to do based on the best use of your abilities.

I do not give one hoot about what "you am." The only thing important is what "you can." Once again, you can do just about anything. People have done amazing things. I can show you people with tremendous difficulties to overcome and yet they still accomplish the most incredible things. It does not matter who you are or how you feel about who you are, because you rarely feel good enough about yourself to do amazing things. The important thing is to know, without a doubt, that you *can* do amazing things. Not perfectly—at least not to begin with. But when you begin by doing a little you can build the courage to do more. And with that courage you can do a little more, and then a little more. And then a little more until it is done and something amazing has been accomplished.

That is why motivation alone does not work. Motivation typically means that some outside force will inspire you to feel good enough about yourself so you will be able to do anything your little heart desires. Forget it. Instead I say that in order to do anything your heart desires you must know you can do anything, because if it has ever been done by anyone at any time then you, too, can do it. No one is special. It is just that some people have the courage to begin and are willing to risk failure and are willing to continue doing it until it gets done.

YOU MUST BECOME UNCOMFORTABLE

Big difference, huh? My approach will not make you feel good. And I know how important it is for you to feel good. But feeling good never got you to do anything. If you listen to a speaker who makes you feel good, I doubt you will ever do a thing. If you listen to a speaker who makes you feel uncomfortable, then you might do something.

For instance, about 70 percent of our society is overweight. Do you believe me? If not, look down. If that does not work, then look around, as it will not take long to find that I am right. There was a time in my life when I was a good 25 pounds overweight. As I gained weight I learned the trick. Just buy bigger clothes and wear a lot of black. That way when you get all dressed up, you can look in the mirror and say to yourself, "You know, I look pretty good!" As long as you convince yourself that you look pretty good, you are never going to lose weight. It is when you are on your way to the bathroom about three in the morning and you catch a glimpse of yourself in the bathroom mirror with your gut and your butt hanging out, and you stop and say to yourself, "Damn, I'm huge!" That is when you are going to do something. Why? Because you are not comfortable with yourself. You do not feel good about yourself. What about when you are walking back from the bathroom and someone you love and trust says to you, "Damn, you are huge!" (And she did not mean it in a complimentary way!) Then, I guarantee you will do something. Because *that* is motivation!

Think of me as that trusted loved one who just caught you walking back from the bathroom and I am the one saying to you, "You are huge!" My goal in this book is to make you uncomfortable. Only after you become uncomfortable will you ever begin to change.

Feeling good does not create change. Feeling uncomfortable creates change. Why do you change your position in your chair? Because the position you are in is uncomfortable and you are changing it to get more comfortable. If you were not uncomfortable in your current position then you would not move. You would just stay where you are.

I want my words to make you uncomfortable. Why? I want you to change. I want you to discover your best self and go for it. I want you to believe in what you are able to do, to create, to accomplish, and to achieve.

I want to give you a focus and a direction. I want to encourage you to do something. I want you to take action. But it has to be action focused on what you really want. Not the kind of action that has you running around like a chicken with its head cut off.

FOCUS AND DIRECTION

Typically, motivation is a lot like blowing up a balloon. You blow up the balloon and without tying the end, you let it go and it flies all over the room bouncing against everything. While it is great to have a balloon all blown up to play with, to really enjoy it you have to tie off the end so you can really have some fun with it. You can use it like a ball, or rub it on your head and let the static electricity stick it to the wall. Or you can tie a string to it and anchor it to something and bat it around. Without tying off the end you have the frustration of just blowing it up over and over and over again until it finally blows out the window or pops. While that is fun to do for a few minutes, it becomes tiring pretty quickly.

Watch people who have just become all fired up and motivated, but they have not been given any direction. They are like the balloon that has been blown up but not tied. They bounce around the room letting out lots of motivational hot air, passing out their "Attitude is Everything" buttons and getting in everyone's way. Yeah, they know all the buzzwords and can quote the jargon, but they have no direction. And just like the balloon, they become tiring after a while.

I watched my son, Tyler, graduate from basic training in the Army. After the ceremony when they were doing their yells and cheers and all that Army stuff, one of the sergeants yelled out, "Are you motivated?" At this point the soldiers all yelled in unison, "Motivated, motivated, down-right motivated, you check us out, you check us out!" When I asked Tyler about that, he said they all yelled that out at the beginning of any task, assignment, or exercise. Now what is critical to understand is that they already knew the assignment, the task, or the exercise inside and out before they started yelling about how motivated they were. To yell about being motivated with no clue about the task would have been stupid. Why get motivated without a plan? They had a plan, they knew how to do it, and then they got motivated to accomplish it.

Can you see that is the way it should be done? You must have the plan first. To get motivated without a plan is stupid. You are nothing more but a balloon full of hot air.

I believe you must have direction: plans, dreams, desires, a picture of what you want, how much you want, who you want, and how you want it to be. You do not need pages of plans; you just need a direction that can be articulated and focused on so you can direct your energy toward it.

Other Motivational Myths

I have already addressed the myths of having a positive attitude and feeling good about yourself. While those two alone are plenty to keep you from reaching your goals, sadly there are many more we have been fed throughout our lives that are just as detrimental. Here are a few more.

YOU CAN BE WHATEVER YOU WANT TO BE

A lie. Not everyone can be whatever he or she wants to be. Somebody has to do the stuff the rest of us do not really want to do. Not everyone can be a model or a professional basketball player or movie star. First, you may be short, fat, and ugly. That knocks out that model thing pretty quickly. And you may have no talent or skills to become a professional athlete or an actor—although I will admit there are plenty of movie stars with no talent who seem to do pretty well.

You can become whatever you have the potential to become and are willing to dedicate the time and effort into becoming, and what you have the talent for. That is the truth—no more, no less.

YOU CAN DO WHATEVER YOU WANT TO DO

Wrong. Much like the preceding myth, it will only lead to disappointment. You can do whatever you have the talent to do. And you have more talent to do more things than you have given yourself credit for up until now.

YOU CAN HAVE WHATEVER YOU WANT TO HAVE

If this were true I would know Salma Hayek much better than I do. The truth is you can have whatever you believe you deserve, and whatever you take action toward achieving, utilizing your abilities, your thoughts, and your words.

The real issue with these three myths is the word *want*. You do not get what you want; you get what you take action on.

YOU BECOME WHAT YOU THINK ABOUT

A lie for sure! You do not become what you think about all day long. If that were true, most adolescent boys would be girls. Instead of looking in the mirror and seeing a middle-aged bald guy with earrings and a goatee, I would look in the mirror and see Heidi Klum.

Instead, you attract what you put your energy and attention on. The real truth is this: You become what you think about, talk about, and do something about. As I have already discussed, it is the combination of the three that makes things happen.

AS LONG AS YOU HAVE A POSITIVE ATTITUDE EVERYTHING IN YOUR LIFE WILL BE FINE

Another lie! A positive attitude does not keep things from happening to you. A positive attitude helps you deal with what happens to you. You will have highs and you will have lows. You will have automobile accidents, experience illness, your roof will leak, and people you know will get sick and die. That is life. It happens to all of us regardless of our attitude. How we deal with it is what matters, and a positive attitude helps.

BE YOURSELF

Lousy advice! What if you are stupid? What if you are an asshole? What if you are a stupid asshole? If you are an asshole, stop being yourself and try to figure out how to be someone else—even if it is just a non-asshole version of yourself.

YOU ARE PERFECT JUST THE WAY YOU ARE

If you believed that, you would not have bought this book. You do not believe that for a minute. We could debate this issue a good long while, but instead let me give you my take on this myth. Yes, spiritually you are perfect just the way you are. God loves you and accepts you just the way you are. I love this thought and find it comforting, as should you.

So spiritually it is true you are perfect just as you are. However, on a practical level, you are not perfect just the way you are. You probably need to change many things about yourself in order for you to be the kind of person the rest of us can put up with.

While God will accept you just the way you are, the rest of us will not. We want you to be nice and reasonable and fairly easy to get along with. Otherwise we will not hire you, buy from you, marry you, or be your friend. And you will grow old while being lonely and broke. So wise up and change.

THERE ARE NO PROBLEMS, ONLY OPPORTUNITIES

Have you heard that? The motivational types love that one. What planet are these people from? I have problems. Period. They are not opportunities. They are problems. And they must be dealt with like problems. Of course these pie-in-the-sky thinkers who say this are also the ones who are out there saying, "Every cloud has a silver lining." Not where I come from. Sometimes the sky is black and all it does is rain and storm and make a mess. And sometimes when it storms like that the only thing you can do is take cover. There is no silver lining ahead; brace yourself for a tornado!

The folks who say this stuff are well-meaning. I know all they are trying to do is to get you to put it in perspective, and that all bad eventually holds some good. But to cram motivational clichés down our throats when we are facing real turmoil is insulting.

A problem is a problem. Hurt is real. Pain exists. These are the realities of life. There is no help in sugarcoating them. While every problem can teach us a valuable lesson, it still needs to be called a problem and dealt with like it is a problem.

GIVE 110 PERCENT

Sure, that will do it. Just get out there and give it 110 percent! No? Well that is what all of the motivational gurus say is the key. I have heard them myself. Some of them will even sell you a little lapel pin that has "110%" on it so you can prove to others what a gullible idiot you are.

You cannot give 110 percent. It is impossible. One hundred percent is all there is. It's the maximum. There is no 110 percent; it does not exist and you cannot give it.

It is like getting on the airplane and having the flight attendant announce the flight is going to be extremely full. No, it is not. The flight is only full. Full is 100 percent. It cannot be more than full. If the flight gets more than 100 percent full, then someone is not going.

This really is not a problem for most folks. Very few ever face the challenge of giving more than 100 percent because most people seem to be quite comfortable operating at about 60 percent. Most people work just hard enough so they will not get fired. If you even approach 100 percent, I applaud you. You are in the minority.

However, while you cannot give 110 percent, I will grant you this: You can give more than you think you can. You always have more to give. But you cannot give more than there is. And 100 percent is all there is.

BEWARE OF WHAT I SAY HERE TOO

Be careful what you buy into and act upon—even the stuff I am telling you in this book. Try it, and if it works, run with it. If it doesn't, then run from it. Dump it and get another book and try something else that *does* work for you.

CHAPTER 6

Your Beliefs Determine Your Outcome

What you believe determines what you have, how much money you make, how healthy you are, and how successful you are. It determines the quality of your relationships and the quality of your life.

So what do you believe? You have a list of things right now you are absolutely sure to be true and that you believe in with all of your heart, mind, and soul. We all do. The list is probably not written down, but it is there. Maybe you never took the time to sit down and really think about your list but that is about to change. I am going to give you a chance to do just that. But first, let *me* tell you what you believe.

"Wait! You don't even know me. How do you know what I believe?"

It is easy. I can always tell exactly what someone believes. I can tell by looking at your bank account exactly what you believe about money. I can tell what you believe by looking at your car, your house, your shoes, and your clothes. I can tell what you believe about yourself and what you think you deserve.

Now you may be saying I am not being fair. Sure I am. And you may be saying I am focusing only on the material things to evaluate what I believe. Okay, that is fair. But I can also tell what you believe by taking a look at your relationships and how you get along with others: your kids, your partner, your friends, and your co-workers. I can tell what you believe by how you spend your time alone—what you do when you relax and what you do when you go on vacation. I can tell what you believe by the kind of books you read. I can tell what you believe if you do not read. I can tell what you believe by the television programs you watch and the movies you see. In other words, everything about you—what you do, how you talk, what you have, where you go—all tell me exactly what you believe. Your beliefs always show up in your life. Without exception, you always manifest your belief system.

Your Beliefs Determine
What You Have

What you believe about money determines how much you have. What you believe about women determines how you treat your wife and how you get along with her. Likewise, what you believe about men determines how you treat your husband and how you get along with him. And what you believe about men and women determines how you treat your son, your daughter, your co-workers, and the strangers you meet. It determines how you vote and how you feel about the people you do business with.

What you believe about yourself determines how you dress— whether your clothes are clean and fashionable and whether you

What I Believe

Life is simple.

You create your life: the good and the bad.

Love, service, and giving must be the motives of your life.

Money is easy and comes to you as the result of serving others.

Service often comes disguised as work.

You can be healthy and do not have to suffer sickness.

You live the life you choose to live.

You can change.

Words are powerful and shape the circumstances of your life.

Thoughts are creative and control your outcome.

Trust your feelings.

Whining and refusing to take responsibility kill your chances of success.

Results never lie.

Most people are lazy and need to get off their butts and do something.

All good is rewarded.

Guilt serves no purpose.

Worry is a waste of time and energy.

Personal satisfaction comes only when you rise above the approval of others.

Everything in life gets better when you get better and nothing gets better until you get better.

When it comes to kids, remember: They grow out of it.

God is the Presence of Good and the Action of Love.

Love your work and by loving it you will become excellent at it and well rewarded.

It is wonderful to have lots of stuff, but it takes more than stuff to make you happy.

Fun should be a way of life, not something you have from time to time.

Everything in life is a lesson. Refusing to learn the lesson means that it will be repeated until the lesson is learned.

In the long run, none of this really matters much anyway so there is no need to get your panties in a wad.

shine your shoes. What you believe about love determines how much of it you give and receive. What you believe about success determines how much of you have. What you believe about happiness determines if you are or not.

Now do you see how I can tell you exactly what you believe by just looking at you and your stuff? Your beliefs leave a trail that shows up in every area of your life.

Look at your life. Take some time to consider the way you live. Think about your belief system and how it affects your possessions, your relationships, your success, and your happiness. Maybe for the first time ever, you'll know why your life is the way it is.

"Most of the shadows of this life are caused by our standing in our own sunshine."

—Ralph Waldo Emerson

As you may realize by now, I am big on lists. In a moment I want you to make a list of what you believe, but first you can look at my list on the preceding page to see what I believe.

That is what I believe. Now make your own list about what you believe on the page that follows.

After making your list, do you see how what you believe has affected your results? Look at your life and try to determine what belief you have that has created and supported that result. If you are not happy with your results, change your beliefs.

What I Believe

_____

_____

_____

_____

_____

_____

_____

_____

_____

_____

_____

_____

_____

_____

_____

_____

_____

_____

_____

_____

CHAPTER 7

The Enjoyment Factor

"All of the animals except man know that the principal business of life is to enjoy it."

—Samuel Butler

My guess is you are not having as much fun as you should have and certainly not as much fun as you could have. If you are like most people, you do not really think your job is fun, but you tolerate it or do it because you think you have to or need to. You probably do not think your friends are all that much fun, but it just seems like too much effort to find new ones. You might not even enjoy your spouse all that much either. Maybe you do not enjoy how you dress, the car you drive, or the house you live in. And there is a very good chance you do not enjoy how you look.

If I am even close to right with any of these statements, then you need to hear this! I want to change your thinking about enjoying life. I want you to enjoy every aspect of your life. You can submit to total enjoyment and make more money, have better relationships, be more successful, and have more fun than ever before.

Stop Doing the Things
You Do Not Enjoy Doing

Why do you do things you do not enjoy? Is it because you think you have to? No, you do not. Is it because it is expected of you? I am not buying it. Is it because you have responsibilities? Your responsibilities are better taken care of when you enjoy yourself. And your primary responsibility is to your own happiness! Bottom line: You do not have to do things you do not enjoy. Really.

> "More damage has been done to others by persons leading lives of quiet desperation (that is, doing what they felt they 'had' to do) than ever was done by persons freely doing what they wanted to do."
>
> —Neale Donald Walsch,
> *Conversations with God*, Book 3

MY PHILOSOPHY OF FUN AND ENJOYMENT

> "God respects me when I work, but He loves me when I sing."
>
> —Rabindranath Tagore

The overriding principle that rules my life is enjoyment. Some of you may think this statement is self-centered and hedonistic. You could not be more wrong. This statement is actually based on a motive of service to others.

Pay attention to this next part. When you enjoy what you do, you will figure out a way to be excellent at it. When you are excellent at what you do, you will serve others better by doing it well. When you serve others well, you will be rewarded well.

In other words, your success is a result of how well you serve others. How much money you have depends on how well you serve others. Do you have much money? No? Then you probably are not serving very well. And when you are rewarded well, you will have more to share with others.

"Give yourself abundant pleasure, and you will have abundant pleasure to give others."
— Neale Donald Walsch,
Conversations with God, Book 2

WHY ENJOYMENT IS SO IMPORTANT

An absence of enjoyment indicates a presence of frustration and dissatisfaction. Dissatisfaction and frustration lead to negativity. Negativity in your life means you will react negatively to everyone and everything you come in contact with. That means you are ultimately going to screw up your relationships at home and at work. You will be a jerk to your family. You will be a creep to your coworkers and your customers. You will probably make your boss mad. In the end, you get fired, you lose all your friends, and your spouse or partner will dump you and take all your stuff. You will end up lonely and broke.

Think I am exaggerating? Maybe, though probably not by much. Actually I am just accelerating the process to show you what happens when you do not enjoy yourself and do not enjoy what you do.

Your Job.   Do you enjoy your job? If not, then quit.
"But, but, but. . . ."
No buts about it. Quit. If you do not enjoy what you do, then you probably are not any good at it. If you are not any good at it, then you are probably not one of those "in favor" where you work. And when

you go home you are miserable and do nothing but gripe and complain, which is not fair to your family.

So either quit your job and find another one or learn to enjoy the job you have. In fact, before you quit, try that. Think about what you do enjoy about your job and focus on that for a while. What you focus on, expands. You may find out that given a chance, it is a pretty good job after all. I admit that no matter what you do, there will be some aspect of it that is not as enjoyable as other aspects. However, I will not back down from the idea that overall you must enjoy your job.

> **"There is no scarcity of opportunity to make a living at what you love. There's only a scarcity of resolve to make it happen."**
>
> **—Dr. Wayne Dyer**

If you do something you do not like doing for the sake of others, then you just end up resenting those people for keeping you from doing what you like.

One of the smallest groups I ever spoke to had eleven people. There were ten vice-presidents and one president in the meeting. I made the statement, "When it quits being fun you ought to quit." I took a breath and reached for a drink of water before continuing when one of the vice-presidents interrupted me and said, "Just a minute, Larry—I quit." At that point he stood up and walked out of the meeting. Now that will put a damper on a seminar in a hurry! I suggested we take a short break. After the break, the president of the company came up to me and told me not to say anything like that again. How sad that a man has to become so frustrated with his job he is willing to quit under those circumstances. Can you imagine what he must have been dealing with to quit at that moment and in that way? He later wrote me a letter and told me that after my statement, he felt he had finally been given permission to stop doing what he hated. So he took action.

> "If we just do what we love, love what we do, and express ourselves freely, we are serving others in accordance to our purpose. All that is left is for us to open ourselves to receive."
>
> —Arnold Patent

Your Friends.   Do you enjoy your friends? If not, dump them. Seriously. I am not even going to talk very much about this one. Why spend time with people you do not enjoy? There are plenty of people out there (about 6 billion), so surely you can find a handful of people you enjoy spending time with. I have a personal policy that I will not spend time with people I do not enjoy. That means I do not go to parties or to dinner with people I do not really like. At times that makes me very unpopular with others including my wife, but very popular with myself. I just will not compromise my personal happiness to put myself in the presence of people I do not like. Selfish? You bet! And I suggest everyone do it.

Your Spouse, Partner, or Significant Other.   Do you enjoy your spouse, partner or significant other? What are you doing about it? Have you tried? If you have honestly tried and it is just not working, then move on. Again, life is too short to spend it with someone you do not enjoy. If he or she does not make your heart soar, move on.

Am I suggesting divorce? Yes. Divorce is better than unhappiness. And do not give me the thing about the kids. No kid ought to have an unhappy relationship as a role model.

If you are not legally married and do not enjoy the person you are with, there is no reason to even have a discussion about this. Just move out and move on.

Does this sound harsh to you? It is harsh compared to all those whiney books about the planets (only you enlightened ones will get that) that talk about relationships. But sometimes people stay way too long in a bad relationship. If you find yourself in one, then fix it. Do not bother with who made it bad, and trust me on this one, both of you did. Blaming will not fix it. Get honest with each other. Talk openly about the way you feel and find out how your partner feels. Get help from a third party. Try a little time apart. Distance cools tempers and resentment and provides perspective. Work on it apart and together and with someone else. Then, if it still does not do it for you, if you cannot be happy together, get out.

No one benefits from a bad relationship. No one.

> "Taking a conscious stand for enjoyment is very important, because many of us have strong beliefs that relationships have to be effortful, painful, and difficult."
>
> —Gay Hendricks

Your Stuff.   Do you enjoy your house? If not, then move. Cannot afford to move? Paint the house. Cannot afford to paint it? Move the furniture around.

Do you like your car? Then why are you still driving it? Sell it or trade it. Cannot afford to? Then buy a bicycle or ride the bus!

Do you not like what you wear? Buy something different to wear. Cannot afford it? Go to the thrift store. The clothes are cheap, and even the stars shop there.

Do you not like your furniture? Garage sale time.

Do you not enjoy the town you live in? Move. I know that sounds drastic. Sometimes it is. It is not easy to just pick up and move. I used to live in Tulsa, Oklahoma. I was born in Oklahoma and while I had lived in other places, I ended up there because of family. We all do things like that. We live for others instead of ourselves and we end up unhappy and resentful. Living in Tulsa did not have me at the point of resentment or unhappiness, but I just was not crazy-in-love with the city. Mostly it was the weather. I hate cold weather. My wife, Rose Mary, hates it even more. So I did this little calculation. I was 45 years old. I figured I had about 30 good years left to live if things went pretty well for me. I loved Tulsa four months out of the year. It is a gorgeous place. The weather, the azaleas . . . it is just amazing. The other eight months it is just too cold, or too hot and humid for me. I figured out that I loved where I lived one-third of every year. The other two-thirds were not good for me. When I applied that two-thirds percentage to the balance of my life I realized I would not like where I was living for 20 years of my next 30. I did not like the odds. So I moved to Arizona where I love it ten months out of the year and stay inside the other two months—because it is so hot, dogs explode and burst into flames just walking down the street.

Was it hard? Of course it was hard. I left behind my family and my business and my employees and all I was familiar with. Was it worth it? Absolutely. There is something very gratifying about waking up every day and loving where you live.

Your Appearance.   Do you enjoy your appearance? If not, then change it.

There are things you can do to make you feel better about your appearance:

Get your hair styled differently.
Change the color of your hair.
Get a nose job if you have a big honker.

If your head looks like a '67 Coupe de Ville with the doors open, then get your ears pinned.

Lose some weight, or gain some weight (though I estimate that there are only .001 percent of you that gaining weight applies to.)

Get cosmetic surgery if you want to. It is your body and up to you to do what it takes to make you feel good about yourself.

Do whatever it takes to feel good about your appearance. But please, guys, do not buy a rug. Unless you can afford one that looks like the one Burt Reynolds wears, then you will look like Davy Crockett in a coonskin cap—regardless of what the salesperson tells you. Trust me, we can tell. Always. And we will laugh; if not to your face, then behind your back.

SOME IRONY: ENJOY THE WAY THINGS ARE

"What?"

Listen to me here. Learn to enjoy things just the way they are. I know it sounds like just the opposite of everything that I have said up until now, but it is not.

"How can you say that? First you say that I must enjoy my life and everything in it and if I don't, then I need to change it. Then when I decide to change my life because I don't enjoy it, you tell me that I am supposed to enjoy it just the way it is! Make up your mind!"

I am not saying things should stay the way they are. I am just saying you should learn to enjoy the way things are while you are in the process of changing them.

Do not become so frustrated by the idea of changing your life so you can enjoy it more, that you forget to enjoy it right now. It is not about the destination; it is about the journey. The way things are right now for you is exactly the way it needs to be for you.

You might not enjoy things the way they are at the moment, but you are there for a reason. Several years ago I went bankrupt and lost everything. Believe me, there was nothing in that experience that was enjoyable. It was embarrassing. It was demeaning. I lost all my stuff. It was the pits! I did not really mind losing all the money, but I hated losing all my stuff. But it was exactly where I needed to be and what I needed to have happen. I needed the lesson. It was a tough lesson to learn and hard to come to grips with the fact I needed it to happen. But if it had not happened, then you would not be reading this book. That experience moved me onto a path of growth and learning that resulted in my speaking career and allowed me to write this book and experience my current level of success and achievement.

That is what I mean when I say you are where you need to be. I needed that bankruptcy to move me from where I was to where I am. It also taught me to enjoy where I am, regardless of where that is, because whatever is happening to me is happening for a reason. It is there to teach me a lesson. It is a lesson I need to learn to grow to the next level. So I have learned to enjoy the experience in anticipation of the next level.

You may be having tough times. While those tough times certainly are not any fun, there is a lesson to be learned. Enjoy the idea you are going to be better for having survived the experience.

While that may not seem like much consolation, that may be all you get. Besides, when things are tough just remember one of the most often repeated lines in the Bible: "And it came to pass." That is good news! It did not come to *stay*; it came to pass.

And do not ever say anything stupid like, "It can't get any worse than this." Trust me. It can *always* get worse! Regardless of what you are going through, stop and enjoy it. Enjoy it for the simple reason it is not worse!

Other reasons to enjoy where you are are all of those reasons I mentioned previously about what happens when you do not enjoy your life. You know you do not want any of those things to happen, so do not fall victim to whining and complaining. Instead . . . enjoy!

"Be where you are; otherwise you will miss your life."

—Buddha

BONUS IDEA! INCREASE YOUR AWARENESS

Many times enjoyment comes not by a change in conditions but by a change in awareness. When was the last time you really enjoyed some of the simple things in life? If you want to enjoy your life more, then begin by learning to enjoy the things you take for granted: things you probably do unconsciously every day.

"Surely you aren't advocating the old, 'If it feels good, do it' philosophy, are you?"

Yes. Life is short. Way too short and getting shorter all the time. So enjoy it. Become a hedonist and just enjoy it. Stop being so self-righteous and pious and kick back and enjoy it. No one really cares that much any way. I promise. If they do . . . to hell with them! Why do you care so much about what others think anyway? Who are they to judge you? They are not living your life—you are. Get on with *your* life and enjoy it. There is not much time left.

"When we seek money or a good relationship or a great job, what we are really seeking is happiness. The mistake we make is not going for the happiness first. If we did, everything else would follow."

—Deepak Chopra

"We are put here on earth to fart around. Don't let anyone tell you any different."

—Kurt Vonnegut

"Life is too short, and too long, to spend it being miserable. Life may indeed be short, but it is, for a fact, wide. It is high time we started settling for more."

—Jill Conner Browne,
The Sweet Potato Queens' Book of Love

CHAPTER 8

Fitness, Fatness, and More

You do not have to be sick. You can be healthy. It is a choice. My suggestion is that you choose to be healthy.

"Are you saying that I choose to be sick?"

Yes, I am. I believe that you choose, on some level, everything you are experiencing in your life. Even sickness.

Consider the word *disease*. It is dis-ease, or a lack a ease. You are not at ease with your life, your lifestyle, your relationships, and your work. That causes dis-ease or disease.

When you are full of frustration and negativity, your body reacts in negative ways. You will not sleep well. You may end up with stomach problems or get ulcers. You may have migraines. You will accelerate the aging process. You will be nervous. You may develop high blood pressure or heart problems. Your immune system will become affected. Some even believe that negativity results in cancer and other devastating illnesses. I do not have the medical training to be able to prove any of that to you here in this book. However, I am sure of this: psychological and emotional problems always manifest themselves physically. I know that from my own life. When I am happy with what I am doing and with myself, I feel better. I sleep better. My body has more energy and functions better on every level. Yours will, too.

Is this all an oversimplification of health and illness? Maybe. But I like it simple.

Do you believe me? That is fine with me; you don't have to. Just do what I have said all along in every section of this book. Try it; if it works, good. If it doesn't, you haven't risked anything. Try becoming at ease with all areas of your life and see if you do not get healthier.

Past that, there are other things you can do to become healthier. Your health is a temporary condition. It is on a sliding scale. It can and will change in either direction. And except in extreme cases (and sometimes even then), your health can be changed by things as simple as diet and exercise.

I want to make it clear I am not an expert in this area, but I have done some research and I know what most of the real experts say. I know this: Nothing will contribute more to your health than a proper diet and exercise. But you know most of that already, right? Few people really do not understand that proper diet and exercise will help them lead a healthier life. However, many people are still unhealthy. Do you find it interesting we know exactly what it takes to be rich, successful, and healthy and we still do not do it? Why? Stupid, I guess.

"So you think people are stupid?"

People Are Stupid

I was going to save this for another area of the book, but for some reason it just feels right here. Mainly because when it comes to being stupid, being healthy is the place we are most stupid.

So in answer to the question, no, I do not think people are stupid. I *know* people are stupid.

First, let me explain what I mean by the word *stupid*. If you do not know any better, then you are ignorant. If you know better, then you are stupid. Big difference. I will forgive you (for a while) for not knowing any better. The ignorant cannot really help being ignorant. But once you know what you are doing and you do nothing about it, then you are stupid—and there is no forgiveness for knowing and not doing.

If you do not believe me when I say people are stupid, I would love to prove it to you.

STUPIDITY FACTOID #1

We eat things we know are not good for us. Things that make us fat, clog our arteries, raise our cholesterol, and lots of other harmful things. Even after we are diagnosed with these problems and told exactly what not to eat and exactly what we should eat, we still eat the stuff that is bad for us. Stuff that will eventually kill us. Do you call that intelligent? I hope not.

Here is something interesting: According to most religious beliefs, suicide is a sin. Why is it that taking a gun, shooting yourself in the head, and ending your life in a split second is a sin, but overeating and smoking and killing yourself over a 30-year period is not? The end result is the same. So it must not be killing yourself that is really a sin after all. It must be how long it takes to do it.

STUPIDITY FACTOID #2

People put things that are full of carcinogens and other toxins in their mouths or light them up and suck hot fire and smoke down into their lungs. Does that sound like an intelligent thing to do? No, it sounds pretty stupid. Then after being diagnosed with cancer, or emphysema, or some other death-causing problem, they are told that the only way to live is to quit smoking, yet many still continue to smoke. Could you call that anything but stupid?

Of course the simple thing to do is to sue the company that makes the cigarette because they made a product that gave you cancer. How smart is that? They did not give you anything. You willingly went out and spent your own money, stuck the cigarette in your mouth, and fired it up. You did it not once, but thousands upon thousands of times. You must have wanted cancer. The tobacco company printed the warning on the label telling you that you would get cancer if you smoked their cigarettes and you still bought them and smoked them anyway. You knew they would kill you and you still did it, and then you whine about what someone else did to you. Take responsibility for your choices—you made them. Live with them or die with them but either way, know those were *your* choices.

STUPIDITY FACTOID #3

Drink too much alcohol and you cannot drive. Your judgment is impaired and your reaction time is slowed down. All of this is proven. If you have ever had too much to drink you know this is true. Yet, people still get behind the wheel of their car and drive. Sometimes they kill themselves. Sadly, they usually just kill others. Yet they knew they were impaired when they started out. But they did it anyway. Again, would you call this intelligent behavior?

Get the point yet? People are stupid. Humans are the only creatures on the planet that spend every day doing things they know will only bring about their own destruction. People know they are killing themselves by how they eat, drink, smoke, and behave yet they do it anyway. What would you call that? I call it stupid.

In addition, people know they are killing their own planet—the place they live—yet they do it anyway. See any other living thing doing that? No other creature willingly, knowingly, laughingly destroys their environment.

We continually do things we know are exactly the wrong things to do; things that are not good for us emotionally, spiritually, financially, physically, and psychologically. That is stupid.

> **"Only two things are infinite, the universe and human stupidity, and I'm not sure about the former."**
> **—Albert Einstein**

"Okay Larry, aren't you ever stupid?"

Absolutely. I think all of us are stupid from time to time. All of us occasionally do things we know are not the best for us. I am fully aware I sometimes do things that are not good for me. I choose to do them anyway. That is stupid. However, I do not do those things at the expense of health, my success, my prosperity, or most of all, my family. I do not do anything at the expense of those things. Those things are all more important to me than anything else.

I am saying that knowingly doing the wrong thing over and over again at the expense of your success, prosperity, family, or health is stupid. So stop being stupid—in all areas, but especially when it comes to being healthy.

Believe in Health

That is right; just believe in health. In other words, stop buying into the idea you have to be unhealthy. You do not. Everyone, regardless of their current condition, can improve their condition by changing their state of mind regarding their condition.

Stop believing the commercials on television about the arrival of cold and flu season. It is not true. While there is a time of year when people are more susceptible to catching a cold than at other times, you do not have to be one of the people who catches the cold. It never has to be cold and flu season for *you*. The idea that you are going to catch a cold just because the weather has turned a little chilly is a myth sold to you by the people who make drugs they want you to buy. It is marketing. If you stopped buying into the idea of the cold and flu season and quit thinking it is inevitable you are going to catch a cold, then you would stop experiencing the cold and flu season and you would stop having colds.

So am I saying you can just think your way to health? Yes, in many cases that is exactly what you can do.

I have not had a cold in many years. The reason is that I do not believe I am a person who needs to have one. I do not want one, do not need one, and refuse to get one. I am too busy and have too much to do to put up with one. Therefore, I refuse to participate in the experience of having a cold.

Now you might be saying that sounds stupid. Okay, I agree, it does. But it works for me and it can work for you. If you believe it.

MOM AND MIGRAINES

If you have ever experienced a migraine you know how debilitating it can be. My mother had been afflicted with migraine headaches—the kind that put you down for days. She had suffered from them for fifty years. But then, my father was diagnosed with colon cancer. He got very ill and needed her care. She decided she could no longer have migraine headaches. And she never did again.

That is right. She knew my father needed her more than she needed the migraine headache, and she made the decision to stop having them. They were simply a luxury that she could not afford any longer. So she gave them up. Simple as that. She chose to stop having them. After a good long while had passed without her having one and long after my father had died, she told me this story about just deciding she did not need to have a migraine ever again and how they had just stopped.

I was incredulous. That was long before I understood the principles I practice now in my life and am talking about here. I had also suffered for most of my life with migraines, as had my sister. It appears they are hereditary so we all dealt with them. When my mother told me this story, I decided right then and there that I never had to have a migraine headache again either. I told myself "if she can do it, then I can do it!" So I did it. I made up my mind that I did not ever need a migraine again. And I have never had another one. Simple as that. I made a choice and created an expectation, and as a result never had another migraine.

That kind of thinking will work for you, too. If you believe it.

At this point you may be saying that it *will not* work for you. Okay, you are right. It will not.

These are just two examples of how changing the way you think can change your experience. This process works in all areas of your life (which will be addressed later in the book), but do not fail to grasp this concept when you are thinking about your health.

Change your belief system when it comes to being healthy and you will change your experience.

EXERCISE

This is a tough one for most people. They would rather die than exercise. So they do. Exercise programs are not what most people think they are. You do not have to go to the gym and pump yourself up like Arnold.

Healthy exercise mainly consists of aerobic exercise—anything that increases your heart rate for a period of 20 minutes at least three times a week. That is not that tough. A bicycle ride, a walk, a jog, a run, or wild crazy sex for 20 minutes (yeah right—20 minutes!).

I am not an expert in this area, so go to a gym and hire a personal trainer or at the bare minimum get some good books and videos—and talk to your skinny doctor first.

DOCTORS AND HEALTH

Find a skinny doctor who does not smoke. Do I even need to explain this one? Just in case I do, how could you even consider going to a doctor who is overweight, smokes, and does not take care of himself? That makes no sense!

Find a doctor who will suggest proper eating and exercise and natural remedies *before* he suggests drugs. Drugs did not make you sick (unless you are a drug addict), and chances are drugs will not make you well, either. I will bet it was your diet and lack of exercise that made you sick in the first place, so start there.

Does doing all that natural stuff sound strange to you? I find it interesting that cutting a person open sounds better and makes more sense to some people than diet, exercise, and natural remedies. That says a lot about conditioning ourselves for stupidity.

STOP BEING FAT

I have a prejudice against fat. I will readily admit it. I have no prejudices against race or sexual orientation—you have no choice regarding those things. I do, however, have a prejudice against stupidity, laziness, and being fat—with fat being the result of both stupidity and laziness. Those three things are choices.

I come from a big family. I do not mean because there are lots of people, I mean I come from a big family because they are *big* people. Are they predisposed to being big? No. They have poor eating habits and do not exercise. Period. They are not alone. As I have already established, many people eat poorly and are dangerously overweight. I could be. It would not take a month for me to go from fit to huge. I love the taste of everything that is bad for me to eat. Fatty foods simply taste good. The bad stuff seems to have the most flavor. And I love it all. I think gravy and chocolate should be two of the main food groups. But I will not become fat. I will not become fat out of self-respect.

I believe that one of the reasons fat people become fat and stay fat is lack of self-respect. Plus, in my case, I have mouthed off too much to ever become fat. I would lose all credibility if I did not live the way I preach others should live. And putting all that talk out there into the world sets a bar in place that I must live up to. You should try that. Just get real mouthy about something and then the sheer embarrassment of not performing to your own standard will keep you from falling below the bar you have set. My prejudice against fat people stems from my knowledge that I could easily be the same way and have even been close to being the same way a few times, and now have to literally work my butt off *not* to be that way. When you work hard at something, exercising discipline and denial, then combine that with a little sweat, you become very intolerant of those who do not. And please do not think I am fit because I love exercise and love eating right—I hate it. But I hate being fat even more.

There seems to be a controversy going on now about obesity. Is it a condition or a disease? I have watched a lot of news coverage dealing with that question. My answer is that it is neither a condition nor a disease. It is a choice. It is your choice to eat the way you do. After all, did you ever eat anything by accident?

LOSE WEIGHT THE LARRY WAY

There are countless diets out there. They do not work. You cannot go on a diet and lose weight. At least not long term. Many studies have already proven this to be true.

There are only two healthy ways to lose weight: Eat smarter and exercise more. Period. While of course you should visit your skinny doctor before beginning any diet or exercise program, let me give you my nonmedical advice for losing weight and becoming healthier.

- Stop going to fast food restaurants so often. They make their living selling grease. They have to use grease to cover up the fact that they are not serving you much real food. Do not kid yourself; grease tastes good. I like it. And it is okay every once in a while but you cannot do it every day. And do not use convenience or price as an excuse, because those places are rarely very fast and they certainly are not economical.
- Leave the parking spaces close to the door for the old people and the wimps. You need to walk. Park as far away as you can without having to cross a major thoroughfare on foot. (Fat people do not run across streets well.)
- Take your dog, your kid, or your partner for a walk—even if it is just around the block. It is good for your body and promotes conversation, making it also good for your relationship—even with the dog.
- Do not weigh often. If you weigh yourself every day you will get discouraged. You did not gain all of your weight in a day and you cannot expect to lose it all in a day. Do not set unrealistic expectations and then become discouraged because you do not drop pounds on a daily basis. Weekly weigh-ins are plenty often enough to check progress.
- Smaller portions are key. Do not put as much food on your plate. People just eat too much food. I have talked with people from all over the world and one of the things visitors from other countries comment on is that we serve such large portions. No other country can fill a plate like America can. And it seems like the less you pay for a meal, the more of it you get.

We are much more proud of the quantity of food served rather than quality of food served. Go to restaurants that pride themselves on flavor instead of heaping portions. Regardless of where you eat or what you eat, eat less of it.

■ When you lose a little weight, go buy something new to wear that is expensive. You will feel like a million bucks and you will be very reluctant to gain the weight back to the point where you cannot wear your new purchase.

■ When you lose a little weight, go to the tailor and have your good clothes taken in. (I said good clothes; dump the ones that are not so good!) It will make you feel so proud of yourself to actually have things taken in instead of let out, like you have been doing. And when you lose a little weight do not forget to rub your fat friends' noses in it. However, this can be particularly bad if you gain the weight back. So do not gain it back and do not be a complete jerk about the weight you are losing. It is better to eat good food than bad words.

■ Do not think fat, do not think fit. In fact, do not think. If you focus on your weight, it will become an obsession and make you hungry or make you have angst about what you could have done or should be doing or have eaten or did not eat or ate too much of. Simply do what you know is right. Period. The weight will take care of itself.

■ Do not beat yourself up for slipping. If you are absolutely going crazy for a pizza, then eat it. And enjoy it completely. Then adjust tomorrow and the next day. Just do not go crazy very often. Little indulgences should never become regular occurrences.

■ When you splurge, do it in front of a toilet or wastebasket. (I said splurge, not purge! I am not endorsing bulimia here.) This is a trick I learned that has helped me a lot. When I want something like a bag of M&M's, then I buy a bag of M&M's. I open it in front of the toilet or a trashcan and after eating a few—just enough to get the taste and the crunch, which is all I really wanted in the first place—I flush them or throw the rest away in the trash. Suggestion: Use a public trashcan so you will not dive in for them later. I have actually done that! See why a toilet is preferable?

■ Find a buddy to eat with. Not a fat buddy. Not a person who will tempt you with fattening food or take you to places you know you should not be. Instead eat with someone who shares your common goal and will encourage you to eat right.

■ When you are hungry, stay away from places like the food court at the mall and the grocery store. If you need to go out and you know it is to a place where you will be tempted, then drink a huge glass of water before you go to help fill yourself up. Grocery shopping when you are hungry is also just dumb. Eat a great meal and then go shopping.

■ Willpower is totally overrated. I do not have much; I admit it. I have a problem saying no to things I enjoy. Denial is just not my style. Indulgence is more my style. I bet you are the same way. Here is what works for me: lack of opportunity. Do not have things that are not good for you available for easy access. Limit your food options. Do not fill your cabinet with cookies and then try to deny yourself. When eating in a restaurant, ask the waiter not to leave the breadbasket or to bring the dessert menu. Do not tempt yourself.

■ When you stop for gasoline, go to a "pay at the pump" station. That way you will not be tempted to buy a soda or candy bar when you go inside to pay.

■ Drink lots of water. Carry a bottle of water with you all of the time. It will fill you up and keep your system flushed. This is especially important when eating out. Always ask for a glass of water and drink it before you order. Fill up a little so you will not be quite as hungry when you order and will not have as much room in your stomach when the food comes. Then keep drinking the water throughout the meal.

∎ Stop lying to yourself and everyone else. You do not have a glandular problem. The percentage of people in the world who actually have one is so small they do not even count. And you are not "big boned." Your frame may be larger than others but your bones are not the problem; the fat you pack on those bones is the problem. And do not say, "My family is heavy; we are just heavy people." That is no excuse. Chances are your problem is not hereditary. The reason your family is fat is that they eat like pigs and sit on their fat butts. Period. You grew up thinking that was normal. You probably think everyone puts gravy on cereal. It is not in your genes. You probably have not been able to fit in your jeans for a good long while.

∎ Turn off the TV, get off your fat butt and do something. You need to walk or ride a bicycle, or have sex—anything that makes your heart beat a little faster. It does not take a gym or any fancy equipment. It takes movement.

∎ Go to a gym. I know I just said that you do not have to go to a gym, and you do not. But if you are serious about being healthy, then a gym is a must. You need to lift some weights. You do not have to look like a bodybuilder but you do need to build muscle. Muscle burns calories faster than fat, even at rest. It speeds up your metabolism. Plus gyms are full of people who share a similar goal: They want to be healthier.

There you go—my way to lose weight.

Now Let's Get Really Ugly about Your Health

You say you love your family. Okay, I believe you. Well, sort of. Almost. Okay, not really.

Let me explain my doubt. Do you love them enough to get healthy? Enough to do what it takes to live as long as you can so you can take care of them and enjoy them?

Oh, I see, you love them but just not quite enough to give up cigarettes. Even though you know that every cigarette you smoke shortens your life up to 14 minutes according to some experts. What could you do in 14 minutes? Could you play catch with your son? Hug your little girl? Make love to your spouse or partner? Could you laugh together, play together, or just enjoy being together? Think about the last time you really had fun with your family. Remember the very best part of the day and realize that time might have lasted only 14 minutes. Would you give up those 14 minutes in order to smoke a cigarette? You would trade that wonderful time just to light one up? I hope not. Yet every day you smoke you shorten your life and deny yourself and your family the fun and love you share together.

Now on to fat people . . . is that Twinkie more important to you than your kids? Did you really need to super-size the fries? Are you willing to die for those fries? Fat people die quicker than fit people. And even if they do not die, their quality of life suffers because they are overweight. Is a diminished life evidence of your love?

Okay, I have gone too far, right? I have crossed the line. I need to mind my own business. Well, I told you it was going to get ugly.

Heart disease and cancer are the number one and number two killers in our society. Yet they are both diseases primarily chosen to be experienced because people are not willing to stop smoking, stop eating like pigs, or stop sitting on their big fat butts.

How can you look your family in the eye and tell them that a cigarette or the fettuccine alfredo is more important to you than they are? Can you really do that? You do it every time you light up and every time you pack on the fat. You do not use words to say it; you use a fork or a pack of smokes, but the message is still very clear.

Some people even combine the two: cigarettes and fat. It is your choice. But buy lots of insurance — that is, if you can get it. Of course the premiums will be higher. Your family is going to need lots of insurance when you croak because you love them so much, but just not quite enough to be healthy for them.

CHAPTER 9

Everyone
Screws Up

"When you have finished your day, be done with it. Never save any of your load to carry on the morrow. You have done your best, and if some blunders and errors have crept in, forget them. Live this day and every day as if it all may end at sunset, and when your head hits the pillow, rest knowing that you have done your best."
—Og Mandino, *The Greatest Salesman in the World*

Everyone screws up. We all makes mistakes. It is what we do. When you figure out how to live without making a mistake, know you are dead.

We all make mistakes and we all have problems. No one is exempt. Problems are to be expected. It is okay to have a problem, just do not wallow in it.

"But Larry, I have real problems to deal with!"

Sure you do. I understand you have problems. I do, too. We all do. I do not want to hear about yours any more than you want to hear about mine. Neither does anyone else. And it will not do you one bit of good to go on and on about them, so shut up. I get it. You have problems.

But as I have already pointed out, these problems are entirely your fault. You have not done well, because you have chosen not to do well.

You made this mess so either live with it or fix it. But whatever you do, do not complain about it.

Do Not Beat Yourself Up

If you have made a mistake, do not waste time beating yourself up over it. Taking responsibility is not about saying how stupid you are. Instead, just realize you have made certain choices that have brought you to where you are. All you have to do is examine those choices and make new ones in order to be somewhere else.

A SMART KID

One day as I was walking out of the back door of my house to leave on a speaking engagement, my older son, Tyler, said to me, "Dad, I have yet to figure out why anybody would pay you to come and talk to them." I thought, "What a nice thing for you to say!" Then he proceeded to tell me how he had been listening to me speak for years and just did not get it. He reminded me that I prided myself on telling people how simple life is. He went on to tell me he thought I had complicated things way too much. He said life was simpler than even I made it out to be. He told me that he had figured out exactly what it took to be successful. I said to him, "Of course, you do, you are 19 years old, just got fired from your job, just flunked out of your first semester of college, and just totaled your car, obviously you have all the answers." I asked him to share with me what, in his opinion, it took to be successful. He answered me with, "When you mess up . . . big deal. Just admit it, fix it, and move on. Other than that, life's a party!"

"When you mess up . . . big deal. Just admit it, fix it, and move on. Other than that, life's a party!"

—Tyler Winget

You know what? My son is right. It is really that simple. I have given you an entire book about how to live your life and he boiled it all down into just one little sentence. I hate that!

Big Deal.   Have you ever messed up? Of course you have. Big deal! Now is that a cool way to look at things? Big deal. What a relief that is, just to know that when you mess up, you can say to yourself, "Big deal!"

Will you mess up again? Sure you will. What will you say to yourself?

"Big deal!" In fact, say it to yourself right now. I bet you smiled when you said it.

Now spread the good news. The next time someone tells you that they messed up, just smile at them and yell, "Big deal!" Trust me, everyone will feel much better and you will have done them a real service.

Look at what else my son, the prophet, said: "Admit it, fix it, and move on."

Admit it.   Gee, I think that is called taking responsibility. That is the tough thing I talked about earlier—the thing that most people in the world never get. If he gets that, then I have been a good daddy!

Repeat the following affirmation often:

As of today, I admit that my life is the result of my thoughts, my beliefs, my words, and my actions. I can change my life by changing my thoughts, my beliefs, my words, and my actions.

That affirmation is based on taking personal responsibility. It makes it very clear your life is the result of your choices.

Fix It. Actually, most people are pretty good at this one. When we make a mess, we are pretty good at fixing it. Most people do not really make a mess and just leave it. So I will not beat anyone up on this one too much.

Move On. Now this one we need to talk about. People love to wallow in their problems. That is why we have support groups full of people who want to wallow with us. We like to recant the problem, cry about it, hash it, rehash it, talk about it, think about it, analyze it, become introspective of it, meditate on it, write about it, journal it . . . everything but fix it and move on!

So you messed up. Who has not? Name one. Everyone does, has, and will continue to. So move on!

"Are you trashing my support group?"

Have I been unclear here? Yes! I am. I am trashing your support group. I have yet to see one that really helps people by saying, "You messed up . . . big deal! Admit it, take responsibility for it, fix it, get over it, and move on to the next thing!" If you are a part of a support group that practices a philosophy like the one I just described, then please accept my most humble apology. However, if you are part of a support group where everyone gets together and wallows in the misery of each other's problems, then get the hell out of that group now! Dump the whiney losers and find some real friends.

You can circle up, hug, hold hands, and sing Kum Ba Yah for the rest of your life but until you shake it off and get started on the process of creating a new life you are going to remain miserable.

By the way, a real friend will not tolerate your whining. A real friend will not tell you, "That's okay sweetie, it's a tough world out there and you have been beat up by it. You poor thing, come here and cry on my shoulder." A real friend will grab you by the shoulders and shake you and remind you that you are able to deal with anything! He or she will tell you they will help you get over and get past what you are dealing with. They will not judge your mistakes, but also will not tolerate your BS and will remind you that you are in control of your own life. He will tell you that you created your mess and only you can create something better—if you will just shut up and get started!

That is a friend. A friend will help you fix it and move on!

"No man, having put his hand to the plow, and looking back, is fit for the kingdom of God."
                                                —Luke 9:62 KJV

My interpretation of this verse is that once you have made up your mind to move away from your problem ("having put his hand to the plow"), the only way to ever make it to that place of true happiness and ecstasy ("the kingdom of God") is to stop looking back at the problem and stop continuing to live in the problem mentally and emotionally.

Move on! Besides, you want it the way it is!

"What??"

That is right. Things are the way they are because that is exactly the way you want them to be. If you did not want them to be that way, you would do something about it. If you do anything, I mean anything, then things will change!

> "We were deliberately designed to learn by trial and error. We're brought up, unfortunately, to think that nobody should make mistakes. Most children are degeniused by the love and fear of their parents that they might make a mistake."
>
> —Buckminster Fuller

> "There is no saint without a past, no sinner without a future."
>
> —Ancient Persian Mass

> "There is no box made by God nor us but that the sides can be flattened out and the top blown off to make a dance floor on which to celebrate life!"
>
> —Kenneth Caraway

CHAPTER 10

Religion Versus Spirituality: Whose Side Is God On?

There are many ways to look at religion. In my opinion, that is a good thing. In fact, I think anything contrary to that is the problem.

I have a problem with religion these days. Everyone has their own brand and believes that *only* their brand is the right one. Many of them have their own book, thinking that *only* their book is the right one. Some even think that *only* their interpretation of their book is the *only* right one. So who is right? None of them. No, wait. All of them? I'm confused. Are you? Or are you one of the people who think your interpretation of your book is the only one that is right?

I believe all religions make some sense and have some meaning and value for me. I have also decided all of them have aspects of what they say and believe that make no sense and have no value for me. So here is what I have decided about having the one right religion: The right religion is the one that causes you to love people more. The right religion for you is the one that makes you feel compelled to give money to take care of people who need help. (And that is not a preacher with a pompadour hairstyle. He does not need your money or your help ... except with a new hairstyle.) The right religion causes you to give up prejudice and brings you inner peace. It causes you to care more about the world and all those who live in it. Anything other than that is nothing but branding. We should stop beating each other up with our own particular brand and book and instead focus on the true religion that goes beyond brand and book, which is simply to love each other.

Sadly, religion has become less about love and more about money and politics and media exposure. Churches are scaring people away with condemnation instead of just loving them.

We end up playing a game, sort of like, "My god is better than your god." How very sad for all of us. There is only one God but there are many books written about that one God and many names given to that one God. There are also many paths to God. No one book, name, or path is any better than any other. But our religious institutions have taught us there is but one path and it is their path—and it is our responsibility to write a check to pave that path a little better so more can travel it.

Spirituality is more important than religion institutions. Love is more important that chastisement. Acceptance is more important than judgment. Feeding hungry people is more important than preaching to them. (People cannot listen when their stomachs are growling. If churches really wanted to *save* people, they would feed people first and consider their souls afterward.)

Churches should *en*courage (put the courage into) instead of *dis*courage (take the courage out of). Love has the ability to heal the world, but religion primarily fills it with guilt and fear.

A Personal Revelation

I used to go to a church (a major Protestant denomination) that had the congregation recite together a common prayer that included the phrase, "we acknowledge and confess our manifold sins and wicked-ness." What a stupid thing to say! Why would you want to proclaim that about yourself? I have never really felt "manifoldly wicked." I have always thought I was pretty good. Yeah, like everyone, I "miss the mark" from time to time (the true definition of the word *sin*). But I still had a major problem standing and proclaiming to God and all of the others in the church, and mostly to myself, that I was a wicked sinner.

So I quit going to that church—a simple solution. (Except when asked why I quit going and I said I was not feeling all that manifoldly wicked and was tired of telling everyone I was—the explanation became more complicated than leaving.)

I come from the school of thought that says, "What you say about yourself has a tendency to become true." Because I did not want to become manifoldly wicked I just decided I would no longer say it.

That is also one of the problems I have with the 12-step pro-grams. To me, it does not make sense to stand and immediately state: "I am an alcoholic." I know these programs help lots of people, but I still think a more powerful statement would be: "I am sober." The same would apply to the common prayer we were asked to recite. Could we not just say, "I messed up and I'm sorry and I am going to do my best to do better and be better"? Would that be more power-ful? More accurate?

Say what you want to be true about yourself. Proclaim to God and to the world and to yourself the kind of person you want to be.

Are these typical thoughts about Christianity? Hardly. They fly in the face of almost all you have probably learned and believed about religion. And you might be asking what in the world happened for me to come up with these ideas. These thoughts have not come to me from any one source. No one source is the authority. No one book has all the answers. Not even *that* book. No one way of thinking is the authority either. There is not just one way. The ones who claim there is only one way or one book only prove their ignorance. They usually claim that their book has all the answers because it is the only one they've read. Personally, I have found the ones quickest to want to beat me up with their book have not even read it themselves.

A few years ago when Hare Krishna converts filled the airports giving/selling the Bhagavad-Gita, one of them ran up to me and offered me the book. I stopped and said, "I've read it and loved it. Didn't you like the part where Krishna said. . . ." He had no idea what I was talking about and could not get away from me fast enough! Very few have a clue about what their religion, denomination, or sect truly believes. Very few have read their own "book."

The following quote by Ernest Holmes absolutely changed my whole view of God and religion and started me on my own path to discovering my truth about God.

> **"Ignorance stays with us until the day of enlightenment, until our vision toward the Spirit broadens and casts out the image of a no-longer-useful littleness."**
> **—Ernest Holmes, *The Science of Mind***

This quote is much like my earlier reference to that half-full/half-empty glass. Again, what difference does it make? Does it quench your thirst? The same principle applies to religion.

Does your view of God serve you well? Is it working for you? Does it cause you to love people more, help people more, be more accepting? If it does not, then broaden your view. That may mean you need a new "book" or a new religion or a new church.

When you do find a religion that only causes you to stop judging others and to start loving others, I will bet you it does not have either of the words "First" or "Southern" in the title.

How You Define God

Your definition of God may be different than mine. You may think God is a man or a woman or a great energy force. I do not know what your idea of God is and I do not really care. It just is not that important. Really. Not to me *or* to God. I personally believe God is the Presence of Good and the Action of Love. If you believe that, it is fine with me. If you believe something else, that is fine with me, too.

However, since this is my book and you are reading my beliefs and opinions, let me share with you a few of my thoughts on what I believe about God:

- God is not a He, a She, or an It. God is the Presence of Good and the Action of Love.
- God is not a personification but a unification—the unification of all that is good and all that is positive, and all that is love.
- God is not mean or vengeful.
- God does not care who wins the Super Bowl or the World Series.
- God does not think you are special, but thinks that everyone and everything is perfect in every way just the way it is, therefore there is no need for the word *special*. No one is above another.
- God loves you and accepts you just the way you are; there is no need to change in order to seek approval.
- God is not loving. To say that God is loving implies that God can be something other than love. God cannot. God *is* love.
- God does not need to punish you and will not. You punish yourself enough, so God does not need to. We are not punished *for* our sins; we are punished *by* our sins.
- God does not judge. People judge. You do not have to change for God to love and accept you. (However, you may have to change for people to love and accept you.)

- God does not reward us based on our goodness. Goodness is our reward.
- God has lots of things to say to you. But you have to get quiet to hear them. Your message from God is very private and very unique to you.
- God believes in you.
- God wants the best for you.
- God wants you to be happy, successful, healthy, and abundant in every way. It is not Godly to do without or to suffer. It is just the opposite. We are given incredible talents and abilities—each one of us. No one is without these talents and abilities. They were given to us to use. Not to use them is like a slap in the face to God.
- God is more interested in you listening to God than in you talking to God. So many people are telling you to talk to God—and that is fine. I just believe most of us talk way too much. It is more important to listen.

Created in God's Image

We are told in the Bible that we are created in God's image. And while I believe that to be true, we do everything in our power to live in direct opposition to that fact. Because we are also told in the Bible that God is Love. If God is Love and we are created in God's image, then why are we so judgmental? And mean? And conniving? And manipulative?

It is because we are human. But if we just agreed that we are made in God's image, would that mean we would be what God is? So are we agreeing then that God is also judgmental, mean, conniving, and manipulative? Well, that is something I cannot buy. Yet many people worship a god who is all of those things. Which means they have created a god in their own image instead of the other way around. They want justification for being judgmental and manipulative so they create a god who is that way in order to justify their thinking and behavior.

GOD IS LOVE

It is a contradiction to be judgmental and loving at the same time. Can you remember a time when you messed up and were having a hard time and a friend—a true friend—just loved you? And later you realized she did not judge you, she just loved you? Those two concepts cannot exist at the same time. And while we honor that friend for being only loving, we turn around and create a god in our minds that will judge us.

I do not believe that about God. I believe God is Love—*only* Love. Any other attribute we bestow on God is a human attribute that is in contradiction to what God is.

If we could get our minds straight on this, we would stop judging people who are different than we are. We would stop being so critical of others. We would stop being so hard on ourselves and would instead elevate ourselves to the point we really believe we are created in God's image and would become Love personified—which we are. And when we learn to accept it and get all else out of the way, we will achieve peace, happiness, success, and abundance.

> Jesus loves the little children,
> All the little children of the world.
> Red and yellow, black and white,
> They are precious in his sight,
> Jesus loves the little children of the world.

I learned that in Sunday school when I was about three years old. You probably did, too. We sang that when we were little and smiled and believed every word of it. Then we grew up and decided that it was okay for Jesus to love the little children but not cool for us to do it. Actually, that is not entirely true. It was okay for us to love the little children who were red and yellow, black and white, but then we had to deal with the reality that the little children grow up. And loving those grown men and women who are red and yellow, black and white . . . well, that is another story. Anyone can love a child, but big old ugly adults, especially adults who are a different color, are hard to love sometimes.

Many even took it a step further and decided it was not even all right for Jesus to love the little children—at least not all of them. Certainly not those who were born with a sexual orientation that conflicts with what we believe is right. And Jesus surely would not love those who grew up in a Middle Eastern country that hates America, or children who grew up and now wear a turban and carry AK-47s. Jesus cannot love them! That would not be right!

Sorry, but it is religion that taught us that and it is just flat out wrong. Jesus loves all the little children and the grown ups too— whether they are gay, wear a turban and carry a gun, or whether they hate America. You may not be able to love them. But you should give Jesus a little more credit.

Jesus was not white. Jesus was not American. I know that bothers some people, but it is reality. No one group can lay claim to Him any more than anyone else.

And God does not have any preference for one group over another. However, we do not like that. We want God to be all ours. We sing "God Bless America." Nice song. Nice sentiment. But very exclusive, don't you think? What about "God Bless Iraq?" or "God Bless France?" Dickens's Tiny Tim was right when he said, "God Bless Us Everyone."

My suggestion for you about God is this: Discover for yourself. Read lots of books from many cultures and many religions. Try lots of things and ideas and find what works best for you and that brings you the most peace and love and contentment and happiness. And when you have found those things, then you have found God.

"What do a fundamentalist and a lobotomy have in common? They are both no-brainers."

—Unknown

"I have an everyday religion that works for me. Love yourself first, and everything else falls into line."

—Lucille Ball

"My religion is very simple—my religion is kindness."

—Dalai Lama

"People who want to share their religious views with you almost never want you to share yours with them."

—Dave Barry

CHAPTER 11

Get Smarter

On the average, people spend about 100 hours a year reading. Yet they spend nearly 2,000 hours a year watching television. Forty hours a week in front of the tube and only two hours a week looking at something with words on it—how can this be?

According to the American Booksellers Association:

- Eighty percent of Americans did not buy or read a book this year. (Congratulations, by buying and reading this book you are already in the top 20 percent of all Americans.)
- Seventy percent of American adults have not been in a bookstore in the last five years.
- Fifty-eight percent of American adults never read a book after high school.
- Forty-two percent of university graduates never read another book.

Another study reports only 14 percent of our society would go in a bookstore or a library and actually walk out with a book. And only 10 percent of those people would read past the first chapter.

On nearly every corner there seems to be one of those mega-bookstores with a coffee shop and music store inside. So how can it be that no one is reading? Well, it is true that book sales are at an all time high. More people than ever are buying books. They just are not reading them. Actually I think people go to bookstores just for the coffee.

People Do Not Read

A few years ago I did a press run of 10,000 copies of my self-published book, *The Simple Way to Success*. After selling over 9,000 copies, we received a phone call from a man saying he had discovered my trick. I did not actually know that I knew any tricks. He said that pages 158, 159, and 160 were blank. I did not believe him. I checked, and sure enough those pages in every copy were blank. I had already sold 9,000 copies of that press run and apparently not one person ever made it to page 158. That realization did a lot for my ego.

You have to actually read the books. It is great to own them. I love owning my books. But they never really seem to do me much good until I read them.

According to *USA Today*, 43.6 percent of all American adults read below the seventh grade level. And did you know that over half of all high school graduates could not read their own graduation diplomas or even fill out a simple application for employment? How pitiful.

Want to have some fun? Ask people you know to name the last five books they have read. If they can name one it will be amazing. While this may be cruel, it will be great fun for you. Then ask them what book they are currently reading. I bet you nine out of ten are not reading anything. By the way, this is a clue for you: Do not hang around people who do not read.

HOW TO READ A BOOK

1. If at all possible, buy the book. Libraries are great resources for reference material and for fiction you do not care about keeping after you have read the book. But when you are investing in a book that has life-changing information in it (things you will want to refer to over and over again) you need to buy the book. If you simply cannot afford to buy the book, then go to the library and check it out. However, on the way to the library, kick yourself in the butt for being so broke you cannot afford a book! (There are lots of great used bookstores that sell wonderful books at bargain prices. I saw one of mine for a quarter. What a deal!)

2. If the book is yours, mark it up. Write your name in it. Get a highlighter and mark the parts that say something to you. Make margin notes. When you have finished the book, go to the back of the book and on one of the blank pages write the date and then summarize what you learned from that book. In fact, begin this new habit by doing it in this book!

3. Tell everyone what a great book you are reading. This will reinforce what you are learning. It is also a great way to boost your own ego because it is doubtful they have read any books recently so you can be proud and brag that you have. Plus it might encourage them to buy a book and read it.

4. Do not loan anyone your books. "But isn't that selfish?" Absolutely. Actually you are doing others a huge favor. If you loan someone your book then you deprive her of the privilege of marking the parts that mean something to her, therefore diminishing the impact the book will have on her life. Plus, you probably will not get

the book back. If it is a book that really has spoken to you, you will want it back. Instead, buy her a copy of the book for her very own. This is a sign of generosity and exhibits your giving nature and inflicts on her a sense of obligation that might encourage her to actually read the book.

5. Buy lots of books. Go to the bookstores to browse and when a book title speaks to you, buy it—even if you do not have time to read it right now. Have a "to be read" shelf: a stack of books just waiting to be read. Always have a few books waiting on you.

6. Read several books at the same time. I have books I take on the airplane when I know I have a few hours of uninterrupted time. I also have books by my bed I use to relax me and help me to fall asleep. I have books full of quotes and very short chapters, which I read when I only have a few minutes. I have books that cover heavy subjects that I read when my mind is wide awake and can focus well, and books that are light and do not require a great deal of concentration. Have a variety of books available that fit the time, the place, and your mood.

7. Do not hesitate to stop when you find yourself in the midst of a bad book. You may get 25 pages into a book and decide it is not saying anything to you. Put it down and get another. Do not do that with this book, though; wait for the next one to begin that practice.

8. Read for different reasons. Read to learn. Read to lift your spirits. Read for pure entertainment. Any book is better than most television.

What Should I Read?

Here is a clue: Do not read what poor people read. Know why? You do not want to be like them. Read what rich people read. Why? You want to be like them. Is this stuff simple or what?

However, be careful. The self-help section of the library and the bookstores is full of quacks who have written books just to sell books instead of trying to help people. Some of the best-selling books today are total garbage. A best-seller is not necessarily an indication of a great book.

Do not limit your reading to one genre. Reading only self-help books will soon make you immune to the good they can do. So read books on philosophy and spirituality and read great biographies—but also read some junk just for fun, like mysteries, how-to books, horror, humor, and the rest.

> **"People would *do* better if they *knew* better."**
>
> **—Jim Rohn**

IT TAKES MORE THAN BOOKS

While books are about the easiest source of learning in my opinion, do not limit your learning to only books. There are many other ways to get smarter.

Audio Learning. I have listened to more than 5,000 hours of audiotapes and compact discs by some of the world's leading speakers and authors. If you travel a lot and have plenty of road time you can take advantage of this great way to learn. Practically every book is also available on audiotape. Almost all of the great speakers, lecturers, and trainers offer their material on audiotape or compact disc. In addition, you can download audio material from various web sites for a fraction of the cost of the hardcopy and then listen to it on your computer. You can even do as I do and download audio files to your MP3 player. That way you can listen while on the go.

Video Learning.   Another great way to learn from great speakers is to see them on video. This is one of my favorite ways to learn, as I like to watch people while they talk to me.

Seminars.   Your city is probably full of opportunities for you to go hear speakers, trainers, and lecturers deliver high-quality, content-rich seminars on nearly any subject you can think of. The key is you have to go. Pay the money for a ticket and take advantage of these opportunities.

Talk to Smart People.   Finally, my favorite method for getting smarter: ask people who know what *you* want to know, to share what they know. They will more than likely be willing. Ask a rich guy what he did to get rich. Chances are in your favor he will give you a couple of minutes. Do not be a nuisance and do not take too much time. Just ask, say thank you, and move on. He will appreciate your interest and you will have a real-life nugget you can act on. But here is a word of caution: Do not argue with him. When he tells you what he did to get rich or become successful, do not argue and say things like "that won't work for me." I am amazed when people who are not successful feel they have the right to argue with those who are successful. These people obviously do not know what they are talking about or they would be successful themselves. Instead, they should just shut up and listen and learn something. Do not ask a person who is successful or rich to defend his position. He does not have to; it obviously works, as he is rich and successful. Sadly, this is why most successful people end up cutting themselves off from those who are not. They are tired of defending themselves. So if you get one of those rare moments where you get the chance to ask someone her key to success, be respectful, be interested, and be appreciative. That way, she may let you ask again another time.

If you are hesitant to ask smart people questions, then just hang around and pick up information. I do not mean eavesdrop; I mean be around them and learn what they do by observing. Hope that some of their "smart" will rub off on you. I believe it does. Smart people have better conversations than stupid people. Smart people usually talk about things instead of people. That is one of the ways you know you are talking to smart people: They talk about things.

Here is the bottom line for getting smarter: The more information you have at your disposal, the better you are prepared in the decision-making process. When faced with a situation, you will have research you can fall back on that will help you make the best decision you can. You are no longer "flying blind."

CHAPTER 12

Stress:
Who Needs It?

Oooooh, this is a biggy. People love to talk about how stressed out they are.

"Life is just so stressful."

"My kids are stressing me out."

"The holidays are such a stressful time."

"I just can't—I'm so stressed."

"My boss causes me so much stress!"

Heard that stuff? Said that stuff? I am sick of it!

I have colleagues who make a great living doing stress management seminars. Ever been to one? What a waste. Why would you want to learn how to manage something you do not need at all?

I'll tell you what I have learned about stress. It has been one of my major life lessons: Stress comes from knowing what is right and doing what is wrong.

> **Stress comes from knowing what is right and doing what is wrong.**

Got that highlighter handy? Mark that line right now because you need to remember it.

Take a sheet of paper and write down some of the things you believe to be causing you stress. Go ahead, stop right now; get a pen and paper and do it.

Now look at your list. You know exactly the right thing to do about each of the things on your list. Yes, you do. Do not argue with me. Regardless of what you wrote down, you know. In fact, you have probably known for a good long while what you should do, but you simply have not done it.

The problem is that you are either doing nothing or you are doing the wrong thing. That is what is causing the stress. It is not the things you wrote down that are causing the stress at all. It is that you know the right thing to do about them and are not doing it.

For instance, if you are like most of the people who have done this exercise with me in my seminars, you probably wrote down a person's name at the top of your stress list. Maybe it was your spouse, or one of your kids who is driving you crazy. It might even be an employee or co-worker who is causing you stress.

You know what you ought to do about that person. You ought to dump them. Or you might need to apologize to them. Or you ought to tell them you love them. Or you need to fire them. Regardless of the action you need to take, know that the person is not the cause of the stress. It is caused by you not doing what you know is the right thing to do. The lack of correct action is the culprit.

Maybe you wrote down the thing I find to be the second most popular cause of stress: your weight. Again, you know exactly the right thing to do about your weight. Stop eating like a pig. Start exercising. Very simple. Your weight is not causing you any stress at all. The stress you feel is caused by the fact you know you need to stop eating like a pig and you should get off your butt and exercise, and you are not doing it!

See how it works? Go through this process with each of the things on your list. Then deal with what you know is the right thing to do. Take action to remedy the situation. It may be painful, expensive, or even embarrassing. It will not be easy. However, as hard as it may be to deal with, it will still be much easier than living with the stress.

CHAPTER 13

Learn to Relax

I am not good at relaxing. I am certainly better at it than I used to be, but still not as good at it as I should be. I do not have much time at home and it is hard for me to gear down after several days of traveling. I get a little frustrated knowing I have to squeeze all of the things I want to do at home into the few days I have. I always feel rushed, and rushed is not relaxed.

For some of us, the ability to relax must be learned. That is not a problem for everyone, for sure. In fact, just the opposite is true for most. They relax so much they do not get anything done. But people like me do so much they are not comfortable when they are doing nothing.

I have learned one of the key ingredients for being able to relax is to really enjoy where you live—both the city and the house. I live in Paradise Valley, Arizona. I love Arizona. I find the desert peaceful and relaxing and I enjoy the heat. I also love my house. I like it so much I get jealous of my wife who gets to enjoy it all by herself with just my sweet little doggie when I am gone.

Create an environment you can enjoy and relax in, even if it is just one room. My office is that way. I am surrounded by things I enjoy: lots of books, cigar store Indians, Elvis decanters, movie posters, and pictures of people I love. I am completely comfortable and creative there. When I am home I spend lots of time there. Do your best to make a personal space you can love. Hopefully, it will include the city you live in and your entire house. If not, maybe it's just one room, or even just a corner in the room, or a chair—a place where you can let the world go away.

Another way to relax is to find something you enjoy as an outlet. For some it is golf or fishing—some sort of physical exercise. For others it is reading or sewing. For some, great music or movies. For me, it is painting. I throw paint on a wall or a canvas and my mind just goes to another place. It is totally relaxing to me to put a brush in my hand and spread some color around. Find something that makes you feel that way—an activity that relaxes your mind and feeds your soul.

Another thing you can do to relax is to schedule days (at least one day) when you have nothing going on. I mean nothing. No repair guys to interrupt your day, to show up late, and to end up breaking more than they fix. No lunches with friends. No honey-do's. Nothing. And that kind of day must be scheduled. Then you must be firm about keeping to the schedule of nothingness.

The other thing you have to learn to do in order to relax is . . . I do not know what the other thing is. See, I told you I was not very good at this.

CHAPTER 14

Money Rules!

There are people who say money is overrated. Those people obviously do not have much of it. Having money is a lot better than not having money. I like having it. I can do a lot of stuff with it I could never have done without it. So do not ever diminish the importance of money or the joy of having it. If you do, you will not ever have much of it.

"Money is the root of all good."

—Ayn Rand

My Story

You might think it strange that I have waited until the chapter on money to tell you my personal story. Most authors would have told you their story much earlier in their book in order to build their credibility and to give you a reason to keep reading. But my story is based in money so it is more appropriate for my story to come now. I began my whole journey of personal growth because of money—actually the lack of money. Everyone has a motivator. That motivator might be physical or mental abuse, weight, divorce, job loss, or any number of things. Mine was lack of cash.

While going to college, I worked as a telephone operator for Southwestern Bell Telephone Company in Muskogee, Oklahoma. After graduation I stayed with Bell, received several promotions and was making a pretty good living; not a great living, but a pretty good living. Ten years later, several promotions later and several cities later, I found myself in a position I no longer enjoyed and in a city I did not care for at all. Soon after the break-up of the Bell System, AT&T offered an early retirement package to many of the managers. I eagerly accepted, packed the truck, and headed back to Oklahoma. At that point I started my own telecommunications company selling business telephone systems. I had no seed capital and no knowledge of what it took to really run a business, but I did know how to sell telephones. So with a lot of hard work, determination, a dream and the help of some good people, the company grew to become a real success. I started making good money and finally knew what it felt like to be a success financially.

Then, through a series of bad hiring decisions, misplaced trust in a few employees, a turn in the economy, my dissatisfaction with the telephone industry in general, my personal desire to do something else with my life and a bunch of really stupid mistakes, my company went from being successful to a total disaster. The company went into bankruptcy. As the company's founder and president, and the guy who had so eagerly put his name on all those dotted lines, I went into bankruptcy right along with it.

Sad story, right? Wrong. I earned that bankruptcy. I created it. I deserved it. I made it happen. The circumstances that led to it were the direct result of my actions. I take total responsibility. And while it was a horrible thing for me financially, it is still the single best thing that ever happened to me. I learned more as a result of that experience than I did in all of my years of education, and in all of my years of working in the corporate world. I learned lessons that have become the foundation of my speaking career. I learned it is not what happens to you that matters; it is what you do about it that really matters. I learned about the importance of loving what you do. And I learned that being broke is the pits.

I hated being broke. I hated having my car repossessed. I hated selling my stuff every weekend in a garage sale in order to have enough money to make my house payment and to make my child support payments and to be able to eat. (I was like the guy who sold everything he had except for his bicycle, and it did not have a seat or any handlebars. He had lost his ass and did not know which way to turn.)

That was the beginning of my journey; a journey that forced me to act immediately to change my financial situation. I did not have time to wait for things to get better. I had to make them better right then. I also had to change the entire direction of my life if I were ever going to be truly financially secure. I had to study. I had to change my habits. I had to get right in all areas of my life in order to get my income right.

That last statement is the crux of the whole matter. Your finances do not get right until your life gets right. So while I am about to tell you what it takes to get rich, I want to warn you this chapter is really more about you than it is about money. You see, I still do not know a lot about money. Stocks, investments, savings programs, taxes: all of that stuff is beyond my grasp and my interest. I now pay people to know about money. It is not my specialty. I am my specialty. And I know that when I am right, the money is right and I attract it in every way.

TO MAKE MORE MONEY

Unless you are a counterfeiter or the government, you do not make money. You earn money. Interesting how we forget that fact. We say, "I need to make some money!" Forget it. Instead of saying you need to make money, start asking yourself what service you can provide in order to earn more money.

Jim Rohn points out in his seminars that people make $5 an hour because they provide $5 worth of service and it takes them an hour to do it. People make $5,000 an hour because they provide $5,000 worth of service and it takes them an hour to do it. Why does one make so much more than the other? The difference is not the hour; the difference is the amount of service each puts into an hour.

We are all paid for service. But do not confuse service with working hard. You can work really hard and make very little. It is not how much you sweat that increases your paycheck, although all of us could certainly afford to sweat a little more. I drive down my street and see men putting clay tile shingles on the top of a house in the middle of August in Arizona and the temperature is 115 degrees. They are working hard. I can see it. Yet I know they are not getting rich doing it. Hard work makes you tired but it does not necessarily make you rich. Work that provides the most service to others makes you rich.

Make a list of all the ways you can add value to the lives of others: your customers, your boss, your family, your friends, even strangers. Begin now to think of your job in terms of service instead of just putting in the hours. Start focusing on the service and how you can continually add more value to everyone you work with. Do this and you will be amazed at how much better you feel about yourself, your job, and the people you serve. Plus, more money will show up.

Do More Than You Are Paid to Do. Soon you will be paid more for what you do. Some of you are balking at this one. That is why you do not have enough money. You hesitate to do one lick of work more than you absolutely have to. And you act surprised when someone else gets promoted? Are you kidding me? How can you be surprised that the people who do more, get more? Would you reward the person who not only did her job but went the extra mile? Of course you would. (By the way, the extra mile we have all heard about is rarely crowded.)

Get Your Attitude Right about Money. What is your attitude about money? You have a "money attitude" whether you are aware of it or not. You probably got your money attitude from your parents. It has been influenced by your social conditions, your ethnic background, your geographic area, your education, your age, and many other significant and sometimes not so seemingly significant events that all go together to become your personal historical experience in how you think about money. Some people refer to it as having a prosperity consciousness or a poverty consciousness.

A prosperity consciousness is based on your belief that the Universe provides more than enough for you and everyone else to be secure in all areas of life. It is the comfort that comes from knowing that there is an abundant supply of everything that is never depleted when someone takes from it.

On the other hand, a poverty consciousness is based on a belief system of lack and limitation. It is buried in the fear that in order for someone to win, someone must lose. It believes that all abundance, including money, is limited.

Whether you call it a consciousness of prosperity or poverty, your belief in abundance or lack is deeply rooted and has determined how much money you have. Your attitudes about money and about people who have money have determined exactly how much money you have this very minute.

> **"Make fun of the rich and you won't be one of us."**
> —Reverend Ike

So what is your attitude about money? Not sure? Look at how much money you have; that will tell you what you believe about money.

Here is an easy way to know how you feel about money: How do you feel when you spend it? And I do not mean when you are at the mall buying the things you enjoy buying. I am talking about grocery shopping, making your insurance payments, paying your utility bills and your taxes, and giving to charity. Do you drag out paying your bills until the last minute just because you know you can get by with it? Do you grudgingly pay your taxes, griping every minute about how unfair it is? If you have a problem letting money go from you, then you will have a problem letting money come to you. Money comes to you as it goes from you.

Money comes to you as it goes from you.

When you get a bill, pay it with a smile. Do not gripe about it. Do not complain when the mail carrier brings the mail and all you see are bills. Be glad you are a prosperous person who has the money to pay his bills.

"But I don't have enough money to pay my bills. How can I be happy to see them?"

All of us have bills—even rich people. In fact, especially rich people. Do not think that having money makes you exempt from money issues. Rich people have the same money issues as poor people. They face the same challenges; their challenges just have more zeros attached. Money obligations are a way of life. The reality is that many people have more month than money. But griping about your situation does not make it easier. It only makes it harder. Complaining about money drives it away from you. Why would money show up in the life of a person who only complains about it? Besides, you created those bills and it is your obligation to pay them. Willingly. Happily. On time.

Pay your taxes enthusiastically. Have I gone too far with this one? It may seem too much to ask to pay your taxes enthusiastically, but I bet you enthusiastically enjoyed the benefits those taxes paid for: streets, police and fire protection, and more. I know the government will not spend your money the way you would spend your money if given the same chance. I do not like or support all government programs either. There is corruption and waste and a lot of just plain stupidity it seems. Deal with it by voting differently, not by avoiding taxes.

Besides, when you pay taxes, it means you have been making money. The more money you pay in taxes, the more money you have made. I actually had a year where I did not pay any taxes. Know why? I did not make any money. Believe me, it is easier to pay the taxes on the money you have than to pay no taxes on the money you do not have.

Spend Your Money Easily. This is not a big problem for most people, you might think. However, you could not be more mistaken.

"Almost any man knows how to earn money, but not one in a million knows how to spend it."

—Henry David Thoreau

Have fun spending your money. Do not be an idiot about it, but enjoy it. That is why you have been blessed with it. Of course, you should pay your bills and meet all your obligations first. You should save and invest, you should share, but you should also have fun with your money. John Randolph Price said, "Keep your money circulating. If you hoard it for a rainy day, you may have to spend it on an ark."

Remember: Money comes to you exactly as it goes from you. If it is hard for you to open your hand to let go of your money, then it will be equally hard for you to open your hand to accept more money.

"But things cost so much!"

The problem is not that things cost too much, the problem is that you cannot afford them. Do not gripe about what things cost. You cannot do one thing about it. You can, however, do something about how much money you have. That is your real gripe anyway, right? You are not happy with how much money you have and you are blaming prices? Does that make any sense to you? How much money you have is your fault. Fix that and you will not care what things cost.

"But how?"

Pay attention. *First, believe you deserve more money.*

When you believe you deserve more, then you will begin to have more. Again, get your words right. I wrote the following prosperity affirmation when I was absolutely broke. I carried it with me at all times and read it to myself at least fifty times a day. I still read it daily.

PROSPERITY AFFIRMATION

My world is abundant! I am rich and getting richer! I have more than enough money to pay for anything I want anytime I want it. My pocket is always full of money. My checking account always has more than enough to pay all of my obligations. I have more than I need and all that I want. Money is easy! I have surplus money! I expect abundance and success; therefore I get abundance and success. Money comes at me from all directions. Everywhere I turn, there are people there to do me good. My mail and my telephone bring me good news and great wealth. My calendar is always full of profitable, fun, and exciting opportunities. I speak words of love and wisdom. I serve others. I am ready for opportunities to do good for others. I give freely and lovingly of all that I have. I am always thankful!

These simple words helped me. They still do. I believe they will help you, too. They will help you begin to focus on a world based in abundance.

Important Beliefs

You must believe in what you do, the company you do it for, your customers, and yourself. What you do serves others; if it did not, it would not exist. The more you throw yourself into that service and believe in it, the better you will become at what you do and the more you will be rewarded for what you do.

Believe in the company you work for. If you do not or cannot do that, then quit and go to work for someone you do believe in.

Believe in your customers; they have the money. Earl Nightingale said, "All of the money you are ever going to have is currently in the hands of someone else." That someone else is your customer. Do not tell me you do not have customers; we all have customers. You might call them clients, patients, the audience or you might call them co-workers—but we all have people we serve and we need to believe in them. We also need to speak well of them. Remember, they have the money that is going to make you rich. Being mean to them and talking bad about them will not motivate them to share their money with you.

Love what you do and the money will come.

"But what I love doesn't pay well!"

This gives you two options. First, try your best to fall in love with what you are currently doing. I have already touched on this, but it is important to drive this point home, as it seems so many people do not like what they do for a living. Maybe you just need to look at your job from a different perspective. Look at what originally attracted you to the job in the first place. Remind yourself how much fun it was when you first started. Perhaps you need to remind yourself of what you do love about the job you already have. Make a list of all the good things about your current employment. Write down everything you can think of. If you are honest with yourself then my bet is you can find a lot of things you love about your job. Just stop looking at the negatives and instead refocus on the positive things. Then fall in love with those good things.

If you are past that point and honestly hate what you do, then your second option is to quit doing what you hate so you can pursue doing what you love. Now please do not tell me you love watching television and drinking beer all day. Do not be stupid here, as this is serious stuff. You want more money and I am trying to help you get it. Besides, sitting on your butt watching television and drinking beer does not serve anyone and service to others is what you are paid for.

The option of quitting what you are doing is a scary option. I do not recommend that you walk in tomorrow and say, "I hate it here and I quit." Do not write me and tell me you did that and you are not doing so well now. Be smart about this stuff.

First, examine what you love to do. Do you have any talents in that area? Do you have a passion for it? Are others who do it making the kind of living you want to make? If the answer is yes to all of these questions, then find out what opportunities exist for you. Make sure the transition will not cause you or your family to suffer when you quit and start over. It is great to have a passion but do not make others who rely on you suffer for it.

I get a lot of calls, letters, and e-mails from people who want to do what I do for a living: speak professionally. I do not encourage any of them. I do not tell them they should try it. If a person really wants to do something then what I say will not matter anyway. I only ask if they have the talent to make a living doing it. Most do not have that talent. They think they do, but they just do not have what it takes to get paid to do it professionally. Many people can play the piano but few can make a living doing it. Lots of people can sing a song and do it pretty well, though not many can actually make a living as a singer. You may be able to give a good speech, but not many make real money doing it for a living. Make sure you have the talent to do what you love on a level where you can get paid for it. Otherwise, keep it as a hobby.

"When love and skill work together, expect a masterpiece."
—John Ruskin

You may love it but without the skill you are not creating a masterpiece. You are only creating a false hope that will lead to disappointment if you try to do it professionally.

BE THANKFUL FOR WHAT YOU ALREADY HAVE

"The first step toward discarding a scarcity mentality involves giving thanks for everything that you are and everything that you have."

—Dr. Wayne Dyer

"But I don't have much, what is there to be thankful for?"

Just give thanks for the way things are. It does not mean you are satisfied with things the way they are; it just means you are thankful things are not worse than they are. Does that help? I like what Zig Ziglar says, "The more you are thankful for what you have, the more you will have to be thankful for."

"But it's just terrible for me!"

That is okay, I have had it terrible before, too. I have been divorced, lonely, heartbroken, and bankrupt. I have allowed myself to be victimized by terrible guilt. I have hated my job, had money problems, had people close to me die, made some terrible decisions, embarrassed myself, said stupid, hurtful things to people I love, messed up in my marriage and with my kids and more. Does that really sound like my life is much different from yours? Or from anyone else's life for that matter? I doubt it. The point is that terrible stuff happens to everyone. Everyone is an idiot from time to time. That is just the way it is. So it is not special for people to have problems. What makes us special is that we can rise above our problems. It has been said so many times it has become a cliché: It is not what happens to you that matters, it is what you do about it that matters.

Here is a good exercise for you. Yes, it involves making another list. But writing things down with a pen and paper has a tendency to put things in the proper perspective. So play along. Make a list right now of everything that is going right for you. Call it your "Things That Are Going Right for Me" list. Do not try to get too fancy. Just list the things that come to your mind quickly. Do not whine and say, "This is a waste of time because nothing is going right for me." Sure it is. You bought the book. So you had enough money to do that. Write that down: "I have enough money to buy a few good books." That probably means you have a job. Write that down. Even if it is a job you do not like and plan to leave, write down that you have a job—some people do not. Move forward. You are reading this book, so that means you have your eyesight. Write that down. You are not standing, are you? Then you have a chair. Write that down. You are not in the dark are you? Then you have electricity. Write that down.

"Stop! You have reduced this to the ridiculous."

Yes! I sure have. I just wanted to show you how easy it is to recognize things that are going right for you at some level. Life is not a total disaster for you.

At this point feel free to scope up a little as you make your list. Include bigger things like your health. Or how about your car? Even if it is a clunker, write it down. It beats walking, right?

You are on your own now. Close the book and keep working on your list. When you finish, come back to this spot. Really. Close the book. Do the list. This book will not benefit you the way it was intended if you do not do the work I ask you to do. So close the book and make the list.

> **"When we hear somebody complaining that he has not enough, we may know that he has not expressed enough appreciation for what he already has."**
>
> **—Lowell Fillmore**

STUDY PROSPERITY

How do you know what to read? Find out what prosperous people are reading and read that. Simple, huh? It does you no good to read what broke people read.

Read some books about saving and investing. There are many great books out there that can help you decide how to best take care of your money. Interview investment counselors. Find someone you trust who has a great track record with people in your similar situation. However, make sure this person has a lot more money than you do. Never trust your wealth to someone who does not have any. I get a lot of calls from brokers wanting me to do business with them, and I always ask how much money they make. They do not like that—but if they want my business, then they have to answer. If they do not make more than I do, I will not do business with them. Never let a poor man tell you how to get rich. (That is a line you can highlight!)

GIVE AWAY SOME OF YOUR MONEY

Give away some of your money on a regular basis. Please do not tell me you do not have enough to give. Sure you do. Even if it is just a little, there is plenty to share. Regularity is also key. Make it a habit to continually give to reputable places and organizations that meet the needs of people who can use a little help. When you get, give. Do it every time. It works. The more you give, the more you will have to give. It is an amazing phenomenon, but true.

> **"Where there is giving and sharing with no fear of lack, there is always plenty."**
> —Winifred Hausmann

CARRY HEAVY AND LIVE LIGHT

I always carry about $1,000 cash in my pocket. Why? It makes me feel better. Is it that I cannot feel okay without all of that cash in my pocket? Of course not. I feel fine about myself with it or without it. I have plenty of confidence, but I still like the thousand bucks. When I am on stage giving one of my speeches and it is not going well (and believe it or not, that does happen from time to time), then I can always reach into my left pocket and feel that big wad of money and know it is okay if this particular speech is not going all that well because I have a big wad of money in my pocket.

"But Larry, I certainly don't have a spare thousand dollars to be carrying around in my pocket!"

It does not have to be a thousand. Believe me, when I started this practice, it was not a thousand dollars. You can start this practice with any amount that makes you uncomfortable. Yes, I said *un*comfortable. If it does not make you a little uncomfortable then it will not make you feel ostentatious. And that is pretty much the point of the exercise. You have to feel a little cocky—not to the world, but just to yourself. This is your own little prosperity consciousness builder. I started with a $100 bill. Then I moved to a couple of them, then five, and up. You may have to start with $20 or a $50. Which denomination you begin with is not important—just put some cash in your pocket. A bit of excess cash in your pocket gives you some freedom. It allows you not to be burdened by the fact that lunch was more than you expected it to be. Or that you just ran across a great sale and you would really enjoy having that new pair of shoes. Besides, it is not about spending the money anyway. In fact, as soon as you spend it, you will need to replace it. It is about how it makes you feel when you are carrying it.

To me, carrying the money represents getting past being a broke little kid who grew up in Muskogee, Oklahoma, across the street from the Round-Up Club, and raised chickens and picked up pop bottles in order to have some spending money. It is a reminder of what I did to become who I am. It reminds me of the time when I was bankrupt and lost everything and what it took for me to come back from all of that. It represents freedom from my past. It is just a reminder. All of us need some reminders that we have grown. That pocket full of benjamins is one of mine.

Do not say to me you have a platinum card and there is no need for cash. You are so wrong. It simply is not the same thing. Almost everyone has a platinum card—my son has one, and if he can get one, anyone can. It is not about your buying power. It is about your prosperity consciousness.

Cash is king. Always has been. Always will be.

How Will I Know When I Have Enough Money?   You cannot measure your financial success in terms of an amount. No amount is ever enough. The only way to know how much is enough is when you have given your all and done your best. Only your best effort is enough.

Is $250,000 per year enough? Not if your full potential would be to make $2 million a year. If your best is in the millions and you make in the thousands, then you are not living up to the best you have to offer and not realizing your full potential.

Is $20,000 per year enough? It is plenty if you were paid that after giving the very best you have in the service of others. Have you served your best? Have you given all you have? When you have done your best, believed your best, given your best, and served the best you possibly can, then what you have received is the right amount.

CHAPTER 15

Relationships— Friendship, Marriage, and Other Calamities

Let me start by saying I am not an expert on relationships. However, I have read some of those books by people who claim to be experts and I have come to the conclusion they are not really experts either.

Most of the best-selling books on relationships point out that men and women are different—even from different planets. Do any of us really need a book to tell us men and women are different? That is sort of the basic attraction in the first place, in my opinion. It is not just that men and women are different; all of us are different. Again, no need for a book or a seminar on diversity to teach us that, just a little observation and common sense would do it. What we need to remember is that we are alike. It is the commonality we share that will bring us closer together, not the differences. We need to be discovering and celebrating what we have in common in order to have more harmonious relationships.

By the way, I do not really care who or what you are in a relationship with: male/female, female/female, male/male, young/old, person/farm animal or blow-up doll. I think that is your business and the rest of us should just butt out and leave you to it. As long as one of you is not underage, then I do not care. Consenting adults have the right to pursue any relationship that is based in love and brings about mutual happiness. Period. All of us need to keep our moralistic, hypocritical noses out of everyone's business and let people have some fun and find a love with which they feel comfortable. Bet I just lost a few of you right there. But that is okay—these ideas are meant to make you uncomfortable and force you to think in a whole new way. I did not say, "Force you to accept a whole new way of thinking." I said, "Force you to think in a whole new way." You can accept what you want to accept and what makes sense to you; I just want you to think a little. So it is okay if you have a problem with what I am saying—let me finish, then think about it, see if it makes sense to you, use what you like, throw the rest away, and move on. Deal?

There are many kinds of relationships. But almost all of them rely on the same elements in order to succeed. Since marriage is the relationship most commonly dealt with and which most of our civilization seems so challenged by, let us deal with marriage as a relationship first and then deal with the elements of all relationships next.

Marriage

The failed marriage statistics are staggering in this country. Half of all of them do not work and end in divorce. A bad thing? Not necessarily. Marriage is not the end-all/be-all of living a fulfilled life. It is not for everyone. Yet society has implied that in order to be fulfilled, we must be married. That could not be more incorrect. I am not surprised most marriages end in divorce. We have a totally screwed up view of marriage that pretty much dooms it from the start.

We often think marriage provides us with stability. There is not any real stability in marriage. Marriage is like everything else: it is made up of constantly changing organisms that expand, contract, move, grow, and die. These changing organisms, when combined into a relationship, are responsible for the shape and makeup of the marriage. People change, therefore relationships between people must change. That is just life at its most basic level. Things change. It is natural.

Do not think I have a bad view of marriage. I do not. I am only being realistic. People grow. Sometimes people grow at different rates and in different directions, and they end up growing apart. There are other times when people just lose interest in doing the work to maintain a good relationship. There are also times where people become interested in someone else.

This is just reality. The key is to understand that every situation, including marriage, is temporary. You may be saying, "Not my marriage." Well, then you are naive. The only way to have a happy marriage is to have one that is happy moment by moment. You can plan to be happy 10 or 20 years from now with your current relationship, but you may end up severely disappointed.

The best relationships and marriages renew themselves constantly. They do not focus too much on the future. They do not put much stock in the past. Instead, they focus on the now. They put their energy into enjoying every second of what they have at that moment.

Is all of this blasphemous to the marriage vows? I hope so. The marriage vows need to be blasphemed. They are based in the ancient laws of ownership, when women were no better than chattel, except they could bear the children and cook the food.

Marriage is a social contract that imposes fear, guilt, obligation, and compromises individuality. Fear and love cannot exist at the same time. Guilt serves no purpose but to destroy. Obligation breeds resentment. Compromised individuality is the loss of self.

"The trouble with wedlock is, there's not enough wed and too much lock."

—Christopher Morley

I have other issues with the institution of marriage and its abuses.

MISDIRECTED COMMITMENT

Many people are much more committed to their marriage than they are to their spouse. Many people are so committed to the marriage they stay in unhappy, abusive marriages rather than divorce.

If you doubt that, just look around. Do you know couples that are miserable with each other? Do you know people who literally cannot stand each other and only hurt each other and yet because they are married, they will not get away from each other?

In some cases, couples have become so committed to their children that they stay together under horrible circumstances. Children never benefit from being raised in a house run by a marriage where love is absent. In those situations, parents only set an example of a loveless home for their children to use as a role model. They later wonder why their kids have lousy marriages, asking themselves in the woe-is-me voice, "Where did I go wrong?" Where did you go wrong? You gave them a bad example as a role model.

I could walk away from my marriage tomorrow and would not feel a thing. Really. Never look back and smile the entire time. In fact, many times I have been very tempted to do just that. Yet I could not walk away from the person I am married to.

Some of you are thinking I am a total creep right now for saying that about my marriage. But before you judge, look carefully at what I am saying.

I have no commitment to the institution of marriage. However, I have a total commitment to the person I am married to. Which is better? I know my wife prefers the personal commitment rather than the institutional one. She enjoys the institutional one but given a choice would take the personal commitment anytime. I bet you and your spouse would pick the same way.

TAKING EACH OTHER FOR GRANTED

Another issue I have with marriage or any permanent relationship is that people end up taking things for granted. There is much truth in this line from a country song by Johnny Sate and Red Lane, "Ever since we said 'I do' there's so many things you don't."

> **"Marriage should war incessantly against a monster that is the ruin of everything. This is the monster of custom."**
> **—Honoré de Balzac**

For many people being married is like being tenured in your job: you let things slide and start taking things for granted. I do not believe in tenure—not for teachers or anyone else. I think tenure is a license for laziness. And I think a tenured marriage is one that is doomed. The moment you take anything for granted you become lazy. Walk down the street and check out the couples. Look at the couple who were college sweethearts: she was the cheerleader and he was the jock. Now, she is still cute and fit and he has a belly that covers his belt buckle because he is forty pounds overweight. He is now taking his cute little wife for granted. He may love her, may be a great father, but takes it for granted she still finds him appealing even though he has the body shape of the Hindenburg. It works both ways; he does his best to maintain a healthy physique and look good, but she has become dumpy, has gray roots, rarely wears makeup, and thinks getting dressed up means putting on a clean pair of sweats. She has become lazy and takes her husband for granted. She also cannot understand why her husband cranes his neck to look at the hotties in the mall. I could list a dozen similar situations you would instantly recognize, and you could probably do a quick analysis of your friends and know exactly what I am talking about. Maybe you could look at your own marriage and do the same. But like most, you would use excuses like having to work hard, taking care of the kids, and being tired as reasons you do not really take care of yourself the way you used to. Sorry, but that will not fly. If you really cared, you would do what it took to be your best for your spouse. Not out of obligation, but out of desire.

I have even heard men actually say, "What do I care if I don't look as good as I used to—I already caught me a wife." (Funny how stupid words normally come out of people who use bad grammar.) *Caught* a wife? Is she a bass you are not going to throw back? You think once you have a wife, or a husband for that matter, you no longer have to be your best and look your best for them? If you honestly think that, then prepare yourself for a lackluster marriage that will probably end with one or the other of you having an affair with someone who still takes the time and effort to look good.

It is not just looks, though. When you were dating, did you open the door for your wife? Then you still need to be doing it. When you were dating and first married, did you greet him in the morning with a cup of coffee while he shaved for work? Then you still need to be doing it. Did you rub her feet after a hard day? Then you still need to be rubbing her feet. Did you compliment each other? Then do it now. Did you talk about the other's day, or their dreams, or desires, or fantasies? Then you better do it again. If you do not do these things—and believe me, this is a skimpy list used only for example—then you are lazy and taking your spouse and your relationship for granted.

MARRIAGE CREATES POSSESSIVENESS

The marriage certificate is not a bill of sale; it is not even a rental agreement. However, some people look at marriage like a certificate of ownership, saying in essence, "It is mine and I can do whatever I want with it." Legally you are correct. You can do whatever you want with your relationship because it is yours.

It is much like buying a house; you can buy a house, never clean it, never spray for termites, never paint it, never take out the trash and let it build up in the kitchen until it stinks and attracts bugs. You can do that to your house because it is yours. You own it. Not much can be done about it if that is the way you choose to treat your possession. But that does not make it a good idea. It does not make it right.

You can buy a new car, never clean it, park too close to people and get dings on the side, never change the oil, and drive on bald tires. It is yours; you own it and you can do whatever you want with it. But is it a good idea? I don't think so.

Ownership creates two kinds of people: those who have pride in ownership, even to the point of obsession, and those who immediately say, "It's mine and I'll do what I damn well please with it."

Marriage works the same way. I suggest you become one of those obsessive people, constantly tending to the relationship in order to leave it better than when you found it.

Look good for each other. Dress up for each other. Clean up before bed. Women, wear your makeup to bed sometimes and men, splash on some of her favorite cologne before you hit the sheets. Do the stuff you did to seduce each other in the beginning. Put in the effort it takes to keep the spark going.

MARRIAGE IS A ROMANTIC MYTH

"A good marriage is one that can survive the ninety day euphoria of romantic love."

—Edward Abbey

When you marry, you give each other your hearts. Right? At least that is what all the love songs say. Well, forget it; that is a bad idea. Your heart belongs to you. Do not give it away to anyone. Do not share your thoughts all that much either. Most people do not have enough thoughts going for them to think for themselves, much less enough to share. Marriage is about sharing time. It is not about sharing your heart or your thoughts.

She Tore My Heart Out and Stomped That Sucker Flat
—Book title by Lewis Grizzard

Do not accuse me of being some unromantic jerk. I am not. All of us just need to take some of the romance out of marriage for a moment and look at it more realistically. Marriage is made up of two individuals who choose to live together happily for as long as they possibly can. Marriage must be a choice, not an obligation.

Please do not misunderstand me here. I am all for romance. But romance has to do with the quality of the relationship, not about the contract of marriage. We have romanticized marriage to the point we think it is the only way to live happily together.

"Are you condoning living together without marriage?"

Absolutely. You do not know someone until you do. Personally, I believe we should make it a federal law that two people cannot marry until they have lived with each other for a period of one year. Spend a year together, and at the end either walk away with no obligations or get a marriage license. If this law were passed I guarantee we would cut the number of divorces by half. There is no way you can ever know anyone until you live with him or her for a while.

"Wouldn't that be living in sin?"

While that depends on your definition of sin. I think the real sin is allowing people to get married when they do not even know whom they are marrying. And if you are now married or have been married, then you know you did not know the person you married until you lived together for at least a year. As Will Rogers said, "It doesn't much signify who one marries, for one is sure to find out the next morning it was someone else."

The marriage myth is that we will be joined together in perfect harmony: two halves finally being united to make a whole. What a misguided load of hooey. Two people are being joined together in the myth that if only they had a joint checking account and shared a last name, they would be happy.

We must learn to be strong, independent individuals perfectly capable of being alone before we even consider joining together with another person. (Then we should still keep separate checking accounts and probably our own name, too!)

"So are you against marriage?"

No.

"Are you for divorce?"

Yes.

There is nothing wrong with divorce. More people should get one. Divorce is the correct solution to a lot of crummy marriages. (So is counseling and therapy, by the way.) I believe we would have fewer divorces, though, if we reexamined marriage. I believe if we had strong individuals entering into marriage, divorce rates would go way down.

I would much rather see a couple divorce in order to find true love with another person or even to live happily alone, than to stay in a relationship that is destructive emotionally, mentally, or physically.

> **It is better to have a good divorce than a bad marriage.**

Lost you yet?

Okay, I know many of you are now upset with me because of what I have said here. Oh well, I warned you at the beginning. Do not write me. Do not call me. I do not want to hear it. If you do not like what I have said then write your own book about what you believe. You bought this book to read what I believed; now that you know, do not gripe about it. Besides, if you think you are upset now, keep reading.

Here is one more thought. It may not be true for you, but it might be, so consider it:

"The thing you resist is the thing you most need to hear."
—Dr. Robert Anthony

INDIVIDUALITY

In any relationship, you must maintain individuality. Most relationships rob people of their individuality. It takes two people and turns them into one entity. Relationships force us into the role of being two halves instead of two wholes who meet to enjoy their wholeness.

When we enter into a relationship with another person we become a couple. In many cases that is exactly what we become: a couple of weak little people struggling to discover who we are through the life of another person.

We somehow lose ourselves into that dark abyss of pronouns called "they, them, we, and us." It is interesting how we are no longer ourselves to the rest of the world because now we are a couple. Some would say, "how sweet." I say, "how sickening." It is this very type of thinking that ruins many lives. We lose who *we* really are to become who *they* are.

Many couples become linked like conjoined twins—usually at the head. It seems once we are in a relationship we can no longer think without the aid of the other person. We suddenly cannot decide what to wear or what we look good in. We cannot figure out what type of music we like, what food we like to eat, where we like to go, what we like to do, and if we have time to do it without checking with our "other half" or "better half" first.

What happened to us? We gave up our individuality. We entered into the relationship to find ourselves only to end up losing ourselves instead. We are not ourselves anymore; we are "us."

Then something happens to "us." Any number of things. And suddenly, we do not know who "we" are. Is it any wonder? You sold yourself out when you became *us*.

The solution? Maintain your individuality. Stay who you are. Develop yourself as an individual. The better you are, the better the two of you will be. Give each other space. Allow separateness in terms of tastes, space, interests and friends.

> **"The more space you allow and encourage within a relationship, the more the relationship will flourish."**
> —**Dr. Wayne Dyer**

I was once flying out of Las Vegas and seated next to a very old couple. She was seated at the window, he was in the middle, and I had the aisle seat. I was writing some thoughts for this book on my laptop and had just typed the line, "A good divorce is better than a bad marriage." He was evidently reading what I was writing, and leaned over to me and said, "You got that right!" He then went on to introduce themselves as G. R. and Ethyl Griffin and told me they had been married for 62 years. Is that amazing? They had just spent the week in Las Vegas gambling and seeing shows and eating out. They were truly a hoot to talk to. I finally asked them their secret for staying married for that long. She jumped in and said, "I'll take this one." Then she added, "Just let the other person be who they are and put up with it." That just may be the best marriage counseling anyone could ever receive. She told me that after 62 years together they both still had plenty of things they did not like about each other, but they loved each other enough to put up with it. Whole books about relationships and how to have a great marriage have been written with less said than Ethyl did in that one sentence.

We all have these ideas about how we want the other person to be. Chances are, it is not going to happen. People are rarely who we want them to be. (A fact that has bothered me a good number of times in my married life.) People are who they are. Period. No more. No less. Shut up, stop whining, and put up with it.

Someone asked me recently what I loved most about my wife, Rose Mary. Good question, huh? How would you answer that one about your spouse? It was an easy answer for me.

What I love most about Rose Mary is that she loves me. Believe it or not, that is not an easy thing to do and most people could not or would not do it. I am almost impossible. I am loud. Obnoxious. Intolerant. Demanding. Caustic. Sarcastic. Impatient. A perfectionist. A neat freak. And those are my good traits.

But she loves me just the way I am. Regardless. That is what I love most about her—the fact that she loves me. Somehow she can look past the bad things in me and see the good things. What could be better than that?

"The secret of a happy marriage remains a secret."
                                        —Henny Youngman

COMPATIBILITY

We have been told that opposites attract. In magnets maybe that is a good thing, but in relationships I do not think it is so good. Where people are concerned, opposites do attract but not for long. You must have things in common—lots of things. Otherwise you will tire of each other, find each other boring, and begin to resent each other for not sharing common interests.

I think that is why so many people divorce after their kids leave home. Once the kids are gone, they are faced with only each other. Up until that point, their only common interest was the children, but now what is left? In most cases, not much.

> **"Whatever your woman is into, you better be into. Whatever your man is into, you better be into. Your partner into church, you better be into church. Your man or woman a crackhead, you better be a crackhead. Otherwise it just won't work."**
>
> **—Chris Rock**

We have all seen couples where both people are totally different, but if their relationship is a good one, I guarantee it is because they have plenty of things in common. My wife and I amaze people because we are so totally different. She is sweet, nice, conversational, a peacemaker, and everyone who meets her adores her. On the other hand, I am none of those things. In fact, I am everything she is not and she is everything I am not. But other than our personalities, we are very much alike. We both love the same architecture, the same movies, going to restaurants, shopping, travel, books, the same kind of people, decorating, cooking—just about everything she likes to do, I like to do and the other way around. That is what makes it work for us. We share 90 percent of the same likes and dislikes. However, we have very different personalities. (I usually tell people what we have most in common is that we are both in love with the same man.)

And while it is very important to have things in common, few couples have *everything* in common. True compatibility is just too much to expect and mostly overrated in my opinion—even though we have made it grounds for divorce: "We are incompatible, Your Honor, give us this divorce." Better yet are irreconcilable differences. I have yet to see any two people who are totally compatible. And every relationship is full of irreconcilable differences. Few relationships hit on all cylinders. There is always something. One wants sex all the time and one is just not that interested. One loves to travel and the other is a homebody. One loves mornings and the other is a night owl. One loves social events and the other is a recluse. One loves antiques and the other likes contemporary. You get the drill. Think of your own relationship. Are you really compatible in all areas? I doubt it. Do you and your partner have differences that are irreconcilable? I bet you do.

Does it really matter? Not totally. It is okay to be completely different in some areas. In fact, it is to be expected. Not too different in too many areas, but some. It makes it interesting. However, the sex one will be a problem for you if that is the area of incompatibility. A person either has their needs met at home or they will have them met elsewhere. If you do not romance your partner, she will find someone who will. If you do not talk to your partner, he will find someone who will. If you do not have sex with your partner, he will find someone who will. Everyone does what it takes to get their needs met, regardless of what those needs are. This is not a popular belief, but a fact all the same. And if a person does not get her needs met somewhere, she will lead a life of frustration and resentment. But other than sexual incompatibility, the rest is just window dressing.

My wife loves getting up early in the morning. Her eyes and mouth open at the same time. She wants to hop out of bed and run off with a big smile on her face to fix a healthy breakfast while watching the sun come up. She loves hearing the birds sing and enjoys making the coffee and spending an hour with the newspaper. Then she wants to exercise.

I want to wake up about nine or nine-thirty, stumble in to get a big hot cup of coffee, watch a little television and then about ten-thirty or eleven go face down in a plate of bacon and eggs with a side of biscuits and gravy. I will get around to the exercise part after dinner that night.

Is that difference between us ever going to change? I can promise you it is not. It is absolutely irreconcilable. We are totally incompatible in this area. Is it grounds for divorce? I can assure you it is not. It can be annoying as hell, but it is not a reason to dump the marriage.

So what is my point? Scope up. So you do things differently. So you do not like many of the same things. So there are areas of life where you drive each other absolutely crazy. Get over it.

Discover the differences between each other and enjoy them. Make them a source of humor instead of a source of irritation. My whole family makes fun of me for sleeping late. Do I care? Not a bit. I laugh it off while I roll over, cover up my head, and squeeze in another thirty minutes of snoozing. We also tease my wife about her seeing the sun come up. A total waste of sleep time, in my opinion. I saw the sun come up once. I have a good memory and do not need to see it again.

Scope up! We are all different. That is what makes life fun. That is what makes it interesting. That is what keeps it from being boring.

NEED

While there are many lessons to be learned to have good relationships, this lesson has been my big one: You do not need anyone.

Give me a minute here before you totally dismiss me as an idiot. I spent most of my life as a needy person. I needed to feel loved, appreciated, and adored. This was a fear-based belief that was grounded in my own insecurities. As a result of being so needy, I created an environment that fed my insecurities.

I wanted the complete attention of my wife. I got it. I demanded her time, her focus, her adoration, her energy, and her presence. I felt better.

I did the same with my sons. My sons lived with their mother, my first wife. I felt guilty about not having them with me and I became needy to make sure they loved me. I never cut them any slack on visitation so they could have time for their friends or for their own life. It was time awarded me by the court—I had paid for it, I deserved it, I wanted it, I took it.

I also created a similar atmosphere in my speaking business. I needed the appreciation of an adoring crowd. I gave my audiences exactly what they said they wanted. I certainly was not giving them what I wanted to give them. And sadly, I did not always give them what they needed.

This need was very destructive. It nearly destroyed my marriage. It caused problems with my sons. And it made me disgusted with myself because I was selling out to my audiences.

Over a period of time, I realized this approach was not working well for me. No one was happy—not my family and not me. I realized that my happiness did not have to rely on others feeding my ego. I started taking responsibility for my happiness and began to deal with my insecurities. My personal development took me past the point where I needed the approval of others. I had something more important: my own approval. Personal satisfaction comes only when you rise above the need for approval from others.

It first came with my audiences. I stopped telling them what they wanted to hear and started saying what I wanted to say. I started talking about things that were important to me and stopped caring about what they thought of me as a person. If they did not like it, oh well, I probably was not coming back anyway, so it did not matter. I became detached from my need for audience approval. I did not care whether they gave me a standing ovation, a sitting ovation, or any ovation. I did not care whether they bought my books, audios, and videos when the speech was over. I stopped doing things that made me uncomfortable. Things that everyone else in my business was doing—things like conference calls to see what the customer wanted me to say and meeting for dinner to talk to them about the speech. I stopped sending out questionnaires for them to fill out so I would know the key issues they were facing. In other words, I stopped giving *their* speech and started giving *my* speech. I held firmly to the belief that if I said what I wanted to say and believed passionately in, the right audiences would show up. Know what? They did. I got more business than ever. Why? They believed me. They knew I believed in what I was saying. I discovered most people do not believe what you have to say—very few will even listen to what you say—but people will eagerly listen and pay to discover if you believe what you have to say. The audiences could tell I believed in my message of personal responsibility and service to others. Audience approval went up. Bookings increased. Fees increased. Why? The universe supplied me with people who wanted what I had to say because I was willing to release my need for approval. I became authentic. Authenticity in any field is always rewarded.

However, the reaction of many of my peers in the speaking industry was not positive. Many thought that my detachment from the audience was inconsiderate to them. They did not understand the meaning of detachment. Detachment does not mean you do not care; it means you give up the need to control the results. I do care about my audiences. I care enough to give them the very best I have to offer: me. The real me. And the criticism that I receive from other speakers—well, who gives a rat's ass anyway? Are they hiring me? No.

No speaker ever wrote me a check to come speak to her audience. Besides, I figured the best thing I could do for other speakers was to give them an example they could model. I showed them that real success with your audience comes from being excellent at who you are. Only then can you be excellent at saying what you say. Because only then are you authentic. Only then can you "walk your talk."

> "My great mistake, the fault for which I can't forgive myself, is that one day I ceased my obstinate pursuit of my own individuality."
>
> —Oscar Wilde

> "The road to truth is long, and lined the entire way with annoying bastards."
>
> —Alexander Jablokov

Bill Gove, the first president of the National Speakers Association, once said we are not responsible *for* our audience, but responsible *to* our audience.

Amazing advice. Advice that can easily be applied in several areas of life. We are responsible to give others our best, every time, without compromise. However, we are not responsible for others' response or reaction to our best. That is not any of our business. The need to make it our business and to feel good about their responses to us is based in fear, insecurity, and need. How sad to live your life with the constant need for others' approval. Terry Cole Whitaker said it best: "What you think of me is none of my business."

My next level of detachment from need came with my friends and family. As a result, my boys and I have a stronger relationship. I do not need to control their time, their activities, and their thoughts. I have learned to trust them and to celebrate their individuality.

The hardest part of detachment for me was with my spouse. How can you make a conscious decision you no longer need your spouse? It was one of the hardest things I ever did—the most painful withdrawal I ever experienced. Yet, in my opinion, it was absolutely necessary for happiness.

My need for her approval, presence, and adoration absolutely strangled our relationship. Destroyed it really. I took everything she had. I stole her from herself. I completely used her up. Then the day came when I grew to the point that I no longer needed her approval, and what was she left with? Nothing. How unfair of me. Most people thought we had the perfect relationship. Far from it. Appearances can fool you. We were so close, but not close for the right reasons. Close out of need, not out of want. It is much more important to want to be with someone rather than to need to be with someone. Need is based in lack and fear—want is based in desire. We all want to be wanted, but few really want to be needed.

However, that is rarely how it works. People come together thinking two halves make a whole. In fact, those words are ingrained into us with expressions like "my other half." The idea that any of us have another half is absurd. And it certainly does not work when it comes to viewing a relationship. Only two whole people can make a whole relationship. Two people who view themselves as half of a relationship are doomed, because sometimes the halves do not line up. Few people, though, are strong enough to stand alone—confident and whole—next to another strong, confident whole person and create a healthy relationship. Instead, most relationships are based on two emotional cripples joined at the hip pretending they have created one whole, successful being. Wrong.

In the movie *Austin Powers: The Spy Who Shagged Me*, Dr. Evil said to Mini-Me, "You complete me." Similar lines have become popular in many movies where the audience swoons when they are said. It has become popular to need someone to the point that only her presence makes us whole. That is just sad and pitiful. No one completes you. Nothing outside of yourself completes you. As soon as we realize we are already complete and always have been, the better off we will be.

> **"The purpose of relationships is not to have another complete you. But to have another with whom to share your completeness."**
>
> —Neale Donald Walsch,
> *Conversations with God*, Book 1

It is the confidence that comes from the certainty we are okay all by ourselves that will make others drawn to us.

I told my wife one time that when she looks in the mirror and says to herself, "Damn, I am fine!" and throws her shoulders back and struts her stuff I would move heaven and earth to be with her. But when she is being needy, clinging, mousy, insecure, and weak I would move heaven and earth to be away from her. The same applies to all of us. Independence is attractive.

If you go out looking for love because you desperately need someone to make you feel better about yourself, you will give off an aura that will drive away exactly what you want. And if you become independent of the need and just go out to give love instead of receive it, you will have to beat them off with a stick.

> Love one another but make not a bond of love:
> Let it rather be a moving sea between the shores of your souls.
> Fill each other's cup but drink not from one cup.
> Give one another of your bread but eat not from the same loaf.
> Sing and dance together and be joyous, but let each one of you be alone,

Even as the strings of a lute are alone though they quiver with
   the same music.
Give your hearts, but not into each other's keeping.
For only the hand of Life can contain your hearts.
And stand together, yet not too near together:
For the pillars of the temple stand apart, and the oak tree
   and the cypress grow not in each other's shadow.
                              —Kahlil Gibran, *The Prophet*

"Enjoy everything. Need nothing. Needing someone is the
fastest way to kill a relationship . . . the greatest gift you can
give someone is the strength and the power not to need
you, to need you for nothing."
                              —Neale Donald Walsch,
                           Conversations with God, Book 2

"Love consists in this, that two solitudes protect and touch
and greet each other."
                              —Rainer Maria Rilke

The Great Dichotomy.   Okay, let me really confuse the issue. I
have just said that you do not need anyone; no other person can really
make you happy. All true. However, you cannot be happy without
others, either. That is the great dichotomy of life: You do not need
others to be happy and yet you cannot be happy without others.

No one succeeds alone. No one is truly happy alone. We need
each other. We were given to each other to love, to play with, to argue
with, to enjoy. That means we have to figure out how to get along
with each other. A challenge for sure—one I have yet to completely
figure out. But I do have some solid ideas I know will work for you.

FORGIVENESS

Relationships are full of offenses. Two individuals attempting to get along with each other harmoniously is almost a ridiculous idea to begin with. To think there will not be hurt feelings between the two is just stupid. I know you have been told the key to dealing with offenses is to forgive and forget. Does it work for you? Never did for me. If I was able to forgive, I never forgot, which probably just meant I did not really forgive in the first place.

I am not good at forgiving. I do not honestly think many of us are. I like my grudges; I like to wallow in the misdeeds of others. Not very enlightened, huh? And certainly in contradiction with much I have said here in this book. But still honest.

Forgiveness is hard. Especially when you have really been "done wrong."

A Stupid Promise.   My wife and I are not on our first marriages. Sometimes it takes one marriage to figure out what you are not willing to live with before you end up getting it right. Does it have to be that way? I do not know, but second marriages seem to last longer than first marriages in many instances. It seems you are not as idealistic the second time around. Usually it is because people just get married too young. Look at the 21-year-olds you know. Would you trust a person that age to make a life-long decision for you? Exactly! It takes a little living before someone is able to make a life-long decision when it comes to choosing a life-long mate.

When Rose Mary and I got married, I had the words "I'll always take care of you" etched into the inside of her wedding band. Romantic, huh? Then after 15 years of marriage I messed up. Amazing I am admitting it here, isn't it? I know many of you will accuse me of adultery, promiscuity, of being a sinner and any number of things you can conjure up in your mind. That is fine; think what you want.

However, I do not really care what you think of me. I did not do what I did to you. I did it to Rose Mary. What did I do and why did I do it? None of your business. It happened. And in the process of doing it, I stopped taking care of her. I broke the promise I had inscribed in her wedding ring.

We got past it. Barely. It was horrible. We got a good counselor and put our marriage back together. It took years. We cried. We screamed. At times, we hated each other. But we eventually agreed that we loved each other too much to give up on our relationship so we stuck it out.

When things were not going well for us, she took off her ring and put it in a drawer. She just did not believe me any more. I had broken the trust we had between us. She had discovered the hard way that I was *not* going to "always take care of her" as her wedding ring promised.

As a result, a major revelation happened for both of us. No one can take care of you other than yourself. You are responsible for your happiness. No one else can do it for you. Stop relying on any other person to take care of you and learn to take care of yourself.

As we proceeded through our counseling sessions it became apparent we had a real chance of salvaging our marriage. Even though she hated what I did, we loved each other enough to work it out. At the turning point in our counseling, I took her ring from the drawer where she had been storing it and took it to the jeweler where I had the lie removed from the inside of the ring. It would no longer say, "I'll always take care of you." This statement we both had learned was both unrealistic and impossible. I had it replaced with "Love. Honor. Respect." What more can any person ask from any other person? Marriage, friendship, parenting, family, co-workers, strangers— you name it—any time people, countries, organizations, or entities of any type come together those three words should be the basis of the relationship.

I love you enough to want the best for you and to give you my
very best in all our dealings.

I honor you enough to be honest with you, to share my time with
you and to make myself vulnerable to you by sharing the best
of who I am with you.

I respect you enough to hold you in the highest esteem to others,
never degrading who you are or what we have together.

What more could anyone want? What more could anyone
expect?

Forgiveness Is Not Easy.   As I have just admitted, I messed up in
my marriage. I did the ultimate no-no in the eyes of many people.
Then in the midst of my wife's hurt—she messed up, too. No details
here either. Now we were both hurt. But this was different. I had been
done wrong and I was pissed! There was no way I was going to forgive
her. I had cried and begged for her forgiveness and she gave it to me,
but now I could not bring myself to do the same for her. She had forgiven me of my transgressions so why could I not forgive her? I just
could not. I hated what had happened to me. I hated her for doing it
to me. Yes, I loved her, but I hated what she did. And I could not get
over it. I tried. I read several books on forgiveness. I had even written
and talked about it in some of my other works. It was very easy for me
to tell others about the freedom that comes through forgiveness. And
while I could counsel others on it, I would have nothing to do with
real forgiveness when it came to her. That stuff was for those who had
not been wronged as I had been. Their problems were trivial; mine
was personal! It is amazing what hypocrites we can all become when
it gets personal.

So while my wife and I stayed together and did our best to make it
work, it was not working. I brought up her mistake on a regular basis
in order to make her feel bad. I did my best to hurt her over and over

again by reminding her how wrong she had been and how she had hurt me. I justified every bad thing I was doing to her by comparing it to what she had done to me. In summary, the unforgiveness was tearing us apart.

But even more than that, it was tearing me apart. There is no way to be happy in a relationship when you contain anger, resentment, and unforgiveness toward the other person.

The problem was, I did not feel she deserved forgiveness. Yes, she had apologized and I knew she was genuinely sorry. She did everything a human being could be expected to do to let me know she had messed up and felt horrible for it. But it still was not enough for me. I wanted more. I wanted her to deserve forgiveness.

Finally while reading a little book called *The Four Agreements* by Don Miguel Ruiz, I read a line that said sometimes the offending party really does not deserve forgiveness. He pointed out you do not forgive others because they deserve it; you forgive others because you deserve it.

Bingo! That was it for me. I have always believed I deserved the very best in life. I have convinced myself of it completely. However, here I was in a relationship with a woman I genuinely loved and adored and yet I was miserable—all because I could not forgive her. Plus, I was making her miserable and ruining our life together in the process, all because I was waiting for her to do something that was beyond her power. I was waiting for her to earn my forgiveness—to deserve it. I suddenly realized that was never going to happen. Yes, everyone deserves forgiveness. Everyone. No matter what our transgression, all of us deserve forgiveness. But as humans, our humanness sometimes will not allow it.

A great song by Lyle Lovett talks about his girlfriend doing him wrong and he says that God will forgive her. Then the song says, "God will, but I won't and that's the difference between God and me."

While God lives within each of us and we are created in God's image, we are also human. And as humans we must deal with the ego. My ego—my humanness—would not let me forgive her. At least not because she deserved it. But I deserved it. And that was the release I needed. I forgave her because I deserved to be free of the sadness and anger and resentment. I deserved a happy, relaxed, loving relationship again. And the only way to get there was to let go of my unforgiveness. So I did. I forgave her. Not because my ego thought she deserved it. (Though the Spirit within me knew she did.) But I forgave her because I desperately needed to move on to a state of freedom that can only come from living in a relationship based on trust, love, and openness.

Do you have people in your life who have "done you wrong?" If you are like most people, then you do. Are you harboring anger, resentment, and hard feelings toward them? Let it go. Forgive them. Not because they deserve it—because they honestly may not. But do it because you deserve it.

Easy? Absolutely not. Necessary? Absolutely.

FREEDOM

> "Love is freedom. Attachment deprives us of love. Attachment is exclusive. Love is inclusive. Attachment is bondage. Attachment is demanding. Love imposes no demands."
>
> —Deepak Chopra

Freedom is a funny thing to talk about in the midst of discussing relationships. Most think that relationships, especially marriage, are based on a commitment and that commitment takes away your freedom. A paradox: commitment and freedom. Can you have both? Yes.

In fact, you cannot have one without the other. Freedom is a necessity in order to have a strong commitment.

The Freedom to Enjoy Aloneness.   We all need time for ourselves. Time to do the things we like to do without fear of taking away time from the other person. Men need to be able to hang out with their guy friends without fear of repercussion from their wife or girlfriend. Women need to do the very same thing. Luckily, in my life this is not a big problem. I travel a lot so I get time to be alone. Sometimes I really enjoy room service, a stupid movie and no wife, dog, or cat around to bother me. I enjoy turning off the cell phone and isolating myself from the rest of my world for a few hours. Does that make me a selfish person who does not appreciate his wife, dog, or cat? No. It means I enjoy time for me—just me. My wife likes to go to wine tastings and to chat with others about all that stuff. I hate that. I do not do chitchat and I do not want to taste wine—I want to drink it. She goes alone and has a fabulous time. She does not want me there, she does not need me there, and she likes doing this all by herself. She likes to get up early and read the paper. I like to stay up late and watch TV. When I wake up earlier than usual, it interrupts her alone time and she is not happy with me. When she decides to stay up late and watch TV with me, it is not always a harmonious time. Those are times that belong to us as individuals, not as a couple. We do lots of things as a couple but we also enjoy our time alone. We encourage each other to explore things the other can do alone. This is healthy for all relationships. Individuals must have time for themselves.

The Freedom to Enjoy Togetherness.   The marriage vows imply we should hold to each other because we *have to*, not because we *want to*. People do not respond well to *have to*. It is based in obligation. Obligation means we owe someone something. I do not want to owe someone. I never want to spend time with someone out of obligation. I never want to give love out of obligation. I know resentment stems from obligation. I certainly never want to resent the person with whom I have chosen to spend my life. My wife and I are together because we want to be. We have been through too much to feel obligated. Obligation went out the door many years ago between us. We simply enjoy our time together. Nothing is sweeter than to turn down a "better offer" in order to just spend time with your chosen one.

The Freedom to Enjoy Others.   Love is who we are. We must feel free to love others. We must feel free to enjoy others. Do you honestly think it is right to withhold love from anyone? It is not. Love is always good. Love is always pure. Love is always of God. Love should always be expressed.

Now get this straight. I am not talking about infidelity or promiscuity here, so get your mind out of the gutter. I am not saying you should cheat on your partner. I am talking about enjoying other people . . . loving other people. I think it is a natural thing in life to meet other people who you are going to love. And that is okay.

My wife has many men friends—friends she has known for years, worked with for years, friends that I share, and many that I do not. She enjoys their friendship and has dinner with them when they are in town whether I am around or not. I am not jealous one bit. She loves these men. However, they are not a threat to our marriage. The marriage is based on trust. I have the same arrangement. In fact, my two closest friends are women. I do not have sexual feelings for them—yet I hug them when I see them and give them a smooch good-bye. My wife is not jealous, nor should she be. We both completely love these other people who are in our lives. However, we are *in love* only with each other.

Jealousy does not play a part in this love we have for other people.

Jealousy is an emotion based in fear. It is a dangerous emotion that grows from a lack of self-esteem and a lack of trust. It is destructive in every way. It will destroy your relationships and your sanity. Give it up.

> "There's more self-love than love in jealousy."
> —Francois Due de La Rochefoucauld

> "Jealousy, that dragon which slays love under the pretense of keeping it alive."
> —Havelock Ellis

> "When you come to another with love in your heart, asking nothing, only offering that love, you create miraculous relationships."
> —Dr. Wayne Dyer

TRUST

Once trust is broken, I am not sure you can ever really get it back. At least not like it was before the trust was broken. My wife and I do not trust each other exactly the way we did before we both messed up. We are not the same people we were before we messed up so it is impossible to have the same relationship we used to have. Instead, we have a new relationship based on a new trust. The old trust does not work any longer. The only way to make any relationship that has been violated work again is to establish a new trust based on a new commitment.

The issue of trust applies to all relationships. Most people have a tendency to consider trust as a factor that exists only in marriages. But trust is a factor in all relationships: parent/child; boss/subordinate; friends; family members; company/customer; coworkers; corporations/stockholders. Each of these relationships relies on trust. Once it is broken, the relationship changes forever. And in each situation, the relationship pays a price.

Before you lie, steal, cheat, spread a rumor, talk behind someone's back, or disappoint someone needlessly, think about the consequences and know there is no going back. And if your relationship with another has been violated do not think you can repair it. You cannot. You can only start over by building a completely new relationship based on a new level of trust.

COMMUNICATION

We have all been told the key to communication is to meet the other person halfway. It does not work. What if you travel halfway and the other person only goes a fourth of the way? That still leaves a gap, right? So how far should you go when it comes to establishing open communications? I know—how about all the way? Sorry, not far enough. I have been in a conversation where I went all the way and my wife decided to turn around and go the other way. So what is the right answer? As far as it takes. You go as far as it takes to establish open, honest communication. Not halfway, not all the way, but as far as it takes.

Just talk and keep talking, even though the communication may be painful. Silence is rarely your friend when trying to establish or maintain or heal a relationship. In conflict, silence is just easier than having a conversation and dealing with the problem. However, when silence becomes too comfortable, you end up becoming more and more distant.

DISAGREEMENTS

Any time two people get into a relationship there are going to be disagreements. At least I hope so. Can you imagine a relationship where there are no arguments? Can you imagine what kind of mealy-mouthed weaklings those people must be? I do not know who said it but I totally agree with the line, "When two people always agree, one of them is not necessary."

I have heard people say about some couple they know, "There was never a harsh word between them." What? My commentary on that relationship is, "Boring!" My wife and I fight. I scream and she replies in a calm, logical way which makes me scream all the louder. That is what passionate people do. They feel passionate about things and express themselves accordingly.

> **"Almost all married people fight, although many are ashamed to admit it. Actually, a marriage in which no quarreling takes place may well be one that is dead or dying from emotional undernourishment. If you care, you probably fight."**
>
> **—Flora Davis**

It is healthy and natural for people to argue. I actually enjoy it. My wife hates it. I love expressing my opinions about just about anything to just about anyone who will listen. My wife does not enjoy the exchange of harsh words. She would rather keep anger inside and bottle it up. That is the way her family did it and that is the way she was trained to deal with disagreements. My family yelled and screamed and fought it all out. No one ever wondered how any other person in the family felt—we got it said. So for years, my wife would run from confrontation. She thought it meant we did not love each other because we were in conflict with each other. It was a long process to convince her that just the opposite was true. So, she learned to argue with me. We proved we loved each other enough to express ourselves openly and honestly and get things dealt with.

Do not let your anger stay bottled up until it turns into resentment. Do not let the sun go down on your issues. Express them. Deal with them. Get it said and then make up. (Sometimes making up can be so much fun you might want to consider starting an argument!)

The key to arguing is to make it about *some thing* and not about *someone*. Personal attacks are cheap shots and only hurt the relationship. A good healthy exchange about a thing does not hurt the relationship and can actually make it stronger. Steer clear of name-calling. Do your best not to attack the other person. Even if the other person did something you want to take issue with, make the argument about what they did and not about who they are.

ROMANCE AND PASSION

All of us crave romance. And if we are not getting any, we will seek it out—all of us, women and men. That is right, men love romance as much as women do. So learn how to be romantic. There are lots of ways. I am not an expert . . . but I am pretty darn good at it. How? I pay attention. That is really what romance is about. Just pay attention to what your partner likes and then do it for them. It does not have to be anything big. In fact, my experience is that the small things have the biggest impact.

And do not say, "I'm just not a romantic person." Just because you have not been romantic in the past does not mean you cannot learn to be in the future. Never let who you were, hold you back from becoming who you need to be.

> Love can be a huge mountain, a gentle garden, a raging storm, a cool breeze, or a perfect bath. But there is always fire somewhere nearby. There is always the red-hot stuff of the soul's initiation. If there isn't fire, then it isn't love. It

might be a marriage that lasts forever. It might have all the signs of what the world calls a "successful relationship." But if it doesn't insist that you move to your next level, if it doesn't take your heart and make it explode in a million pieces, only to fall back together again in some moment of enlightened understanding, then you haven't really loved. You've done the bourgeois thing perhaps, but let's not call that love.

—Marianne Williamson, *Enchanted Love*

TOUCH

People require the touch of another person in order to flourish. Babies who are not touched do not develop intellectually or emotionally as well as those who are cuddled and held. The same applies to adults. Any relationship where people do not touch will not flourish either.

When my wife and I were in counseling we were made to touch in some way while we argued, even if it was just to touch her foot with my toe. The touch created a bond between us even though all other bonds were nearly destroyed. The touch kept us connected in some small way.

Hug. Kiss. Pat. Whatever it takes to stay in physical contact. Why do you think people shake hands when they meet? It establishes a physical bond that can then be built upon. What is the first thing two people are told to do when they are pronounced man and wife? They are told to kiss. It is a physical bond that can then be built upon.

The first thing that usually goes away when a couple has a problem is the physical contact. That is why our counselor wanted us to touch in some small way while we worked out our problems. When you touch there is an exchange of energy that can heal and bond together two separate entities.

Show physical affection to your partner in order to stay emotionally connected. And remember: Affection that comes from lack of obligation is the sweetest and most meaningful.

A HOW-TO LIST FOR BEING A BETTER SPOUSE

Make a list of everything you like/love about your spouse. Be very specific. Then tell your spouse one of the things on the list every day.

Make another list that describes the perfect spouse you would like to have. Become that list. When you become the kind of spouse you would like to have, you will have the kind of spouse you want.

Leave your spouse little notes saying how much you love him and why.

Find ways to laugh together.

Hug more. Gripe less.

Scope up. Let pettiness go. So the top is off the toothpaste—let it slide.

Treat your spouse with the same dignity and respect you would a stranger.

Fulfill the other's fantasies from time to time.

Do the unexpected. Keep the element of surprise alive.

FRIENDSHIP

Friendship is just about the only relationship that exists entirely because you want it to. It is not like family; you are stuck with those people no matter what. You cannot get rid of them even if you try. Everyone has a Cousin Eddie in the family (remember the *Vacation* movies?). Just duck your head and deal with it. You do not have a choice. But no one is forcing you to be friends. Friendship is always a choice.

You should not have to work at friendship. Friendships should be easy. If you have to work to make it happen, then it really is not a friendship—it is just someone you hang around with sometimes. Friends just accept you and let you be the way you are. They let you have your good days and your bad days. They allow you to be an idiot and make an ass of yourself. However, a friend will not let you whine. A real friend will kick your butt and force you to take responsibility.

You do not need too many friends. That has never really been a problem for me. I have never had very many. It is not easy being my friend—I am what you call "hard to get along with." So when someone is my friend, it is because they really want to be. I appreciate that. I love my friends. I will do what it takes to help them. Period. No judgment. No questions asked. I think that is what being a friend is all about. And it should come easily.

Some people say marriages are like that. They say you should not have to work at marriage; it should be easy like friendship. I disagree. My wife and I never work at our friendship. We work at our marriage every day. Our marriage is sometimes a wreck. Our friendship is always intact.

It is probably better to have a good friend than it is a good spouse. But if you can get them both in the same person, you are truly blessed. So get a good friend and relax. Get a good spouse and go to work.

CHAPTER 16

Kids Are
a Pain in the Butt

Kids are dirty, messy, and expensive. They keep you from doing what you would like to do so you can drive them around to do what they want to do. They are selfish, demanding, grungy little creatures that destroy your house, your car, and about everything else you hold dear. There. It has been said.

Yet they are the neatest things ever to happen to anyone. I love mine. I may not like yours and I certainly do not expect you to like mine. But I know you love yours just like I do mine.

Kids are just so cool. They are always on the lookout for a good time. They eat when they are hungry, sleep when they are tired, and love you unconditionally. And they are your responsibility. You are responsible for what they learn and how they act. Kids act the way they do because they were taught to act that way.

It Is Not the Kids' Fault

You know those little kids you see in the mall and in restaurants that are just so bad? The ones who throw their food, run all over the place screaming, and make everyone around them miserable? The ones so ill-behaved you just want to jerk them up yourself and take control of the situation? Those kids drive me crazy! What I have to remind myself is that the little kids are not bad at all and do not need to be spanked or scolded. There are no bad little kids; there are only bad parents. It is not the kid's fault he is running around the restaurant screaming like a banshee; it is the parents' fault. The little kid does not need to be reprimanded, the mama and daddy do. Little kids behave exactly the way they are allowed to behave—no better, no worse. They push their limits. They are supposed to push their limits; it is part of growing up. It is the responsibility of parents to set limits and boundaries for the child to live within, then discipline accordingly when they do not.

Discipline Is a Must

Parents, you must love your kids enough to discipline them. A lack of discipline is simply a lack of love. I am not saying you should spank them or stand them in a corner or give them a time out. That is your business and there are people much more qualified than I to talk about those things. Just be consistent in your discipline and try to make the punishment fit the crime. And please, please, please do it privately. Do not scream and smack your kid in front of the rest of us. It is embarrassing to the kid and to all who have to witness it.

When I was growing up, my dad would often say, "When we get home you are going to get a whipping." My dad gave hard whippings with a belt. Not abusive and not all that often, but when I got one, I did not soon forget it. It did not matter whether he told me that on the first day of a two-week vacation—when we got home, even though not one more word had been said about it for the entire two weeks, I still got my whipping. My dad taught me a lot with those whippings. The lesson was not just about what I got the whipping for—that was obvious. The real lesson was that his word was golden. A promise is a promise regardless of what the promise is about. Though I did not appreciate that lesson much when I was promised a whipping, I appreciate it now. I learned I could count on what he told me, every time, good or bad. I have tried to teach the same lesson to my children.

The Importance of Your Word

My boys and I play a game based on the idea "What would you do for how much money?" Stupid stuff like how much money would it take to eat a worm? Or bite the head off of a chicken? Just silly stuff we were willing to put a price on and laugh about. (By the way, my price was always much lower than theirs. I know what it takes to make the big bucks and somehow a worm or a chicken head does not seem like that big of a deal to me.)

When my boys were about five and nine years old, we were out taking our dogs, Elvis and Nixon, for a walk. I had some dog biscuits in my pocket and I asked my older son, Tyler, what it would take for him to eat a dog biscuit. He said he would eat one if I ate one. I immediately popped one in my mouth, chewed it up, and swallowed it with a smile and then handed him his. He would not do it. He said he was just kidding.

That is when he learned a very valuable life-lesson: A deal is a deal. I would not let him off the hook. I made it very clear he would eat the dog biscuit just like I did. He made the rules and he was going to live by them. We stood right there in the street for a good long while with him whining about how he did not really mean it. That is when he learned the next valuable life-lesson: Do not let your mouth write a check your ass can't cash. I told him we would stand right there all night if we had to, but in the end, he would indeed eat the dog biscuit.

Finally, reluctantly, he ate it. Some would say after reading that story that I am a harsh father. I disagree. I think it was a moment that influenced his life forever. Now that he is a man, we laugh about that story and he brags about how his dad taught him a lot when I made him eat a dog biscuit.

Few people ever really learn that a deal is a deal and they write a check nearly every day that their ass can't cash. I think they should have to eat a dog biscuit.

What have you taught your children? Have you taught them that television is more important than talking? Have you taught them that cheating on your taxes is perfectly all right because after all, it is the government and not a real person who is being taken advantage of? What do they learn from you when they see you belittle your employees or talk behind your friend's back? Or how you talk to their father or mother? What lesson is being taught with those words?

Your kids are a reflection of what you have taught them. And just like you have always heard, your actions speak louder than your words.

I have tried to teach my children some good lessons. I have taught my children what a good hamburger is and what great barbeque is all about. I have taught them that Elvis is The King. In my opinion, those are important lessons! The rest I watched them pick up from being around me. My older son, Tyler, knows how to take responsibility. When he messes up, he freely admits it and moves toward a solution to fix the problem. My younger son, Patrick, has discovered his uniqueness. He is not afraid to be different and is completely confident in his individuality. Neither will lie—not to me or to anyone else. They say what they feel and let the chips fall where they may. They can be counted on. Always.

Raising kids is not easy. In fact, it is the hardest thing I know of. It is the most awesome responsibility ever assigned a human being. And while I certainly do not know all there is to know about being a great parent, I have figured out a handful of good ideas.

They Grow out of It

This is my number one piece of parenting advice. Every time I got overly concerned about something going on in one of my kids' lives I wish someone had been there with this piece of advice. My son, Patrick, went through a stage when he got his body pierced: ears, nose, lip, naval, eyebrow, nipples—if you can think of a place on his upper body, it had a hole with jewelry in it. I hated it, but I kept my mouth shut. After all, I had my ears pierced and did not have too much room to complain. In just a matter of months every piercing had disappeared. He got bored with it. That happens with kids. Things come and go. The key sometimes is to keep your mouth shut about it and let it slide. If it is something serious, like guns and drugs or something life threatening, then you should get very involved. But a piercing is just not that serious. Pick your battles but do not make everything a battle. Holes grow back. Purple hair grows out. Baggy butt clothes go out of style. Hats eventually turn around so the bill is in the front. Kids do become human again. Thank God.

Besides, as you already know, the more hell you raise about something, the more dead set they are to do it. I think kids wait for you to hate something just so they can decide they like it. It is a game they play with their parents. It is fun for them. Be careful when you play the game because they usually win at this one.

Stay Involved

Know what is going on in your kids' lives. Know what their interests are. Know their friends. Have their friends over to your house for a party. Yes, they will trash your house, but it is better to have a messed up house than it is a dead kid. Yes, I said dead kid. Kids die these days.

There are guns and drugs and suicide and pedophiles to deal with. We did not have too many of those things to deal with when we were younger. Kids today deal with much more serious stuff than we ever did. One of the best ways to fight this is by keeping your kids involved and by being involved with them. Know who they hang around with, know where they go and have their friends come to your house so you can be close—not to meddle in their business, but just so you will be there if needed.

Give Them Their Privacy but Know What Is Going On

Do not read their e-mail or their diaries. Do not be a snoop. You need to stay informed but if you violate their privacy they will resent you and cut you off from any and all information. If you really want to know what is going on, then establish a relationship based on open communication, trust, and respect. Then you will not have to resort to being a snoop in order to stay informed.

Be Cool, But Not Too Cool

Be the kind of parent your kids can talk to. But do not be their best friend. Do not try to be one of the gang. My boys and I are friends but I am still their dad. We can openly talk about anything in the world— and I mean anything. Yet, there is a line between being their best friend and still being their father that we do not cross.

I always think it is sad when I see mothers and fathers trying to be their kid's best friend. Kids should pick their own friends. Let them. Do not be such a needy parent that you require your children to pick you as their best friend.

Be Realistic—Kids Mess Up

Do not expect perfection. Kids are not perfect. They are kids. Especially when it comes to grades. Good grades are not worth crying over. Good grades are not worth sacrificing social balance over. Ask your kids to do their best, help them do their best, then teach them to be satisfied with their results.

The short list for raising good kids:

If you have little bitty kids, sit on the floor a lot. Communicate at their level.

Teach them about money. How to earn it, save it, invest it, spend it, and give it away.

Listen to them.

Ask more, tell less.

Hug more, nag less.

Show your kids affection even after they think they are too big for it.

Teach them the really important things: kindness, charity, love, forgiveness, compassion, respect, honesty, responsibility, and how to have fun.

Never lie to them. Never tolerate any lie from them.

Encourage your children to develop their own uniqueness. Do not try to mold their personalities. Let them be who they are and let them become what they want to become, not what *you* want them to become.

Do not make a jackass out of yourself at their sporting events.

Do not protect them too much. Let them make their own mistakes and suffer the consequences. The lesson is in the consequences.

They need love more than stuff.

Teenagers

Teenagers are such an anomaly they get their own section. They are obnoxious, rude, self-absorbed, pretty much disgusting creatures. There is no known cure, except time. While they do eventually grow out of it, it is always just in the nick of time.

Whey my older son was 16, he went toe to toe with me, telling me he no longer had to do what I said because he was bigger than I was. He was right—he was bigger. But I quickly reminded him I was smarter, I had all the money, and I knew where he slept. I told him I did not see any cure for our relationship except euthanasia; we were just going to have to put him to sleep. I loved him. I just could not stand him.

Have you been there with your kids? If not, chances are you will be. Few kids are immune to being a teenager.

My only advice for you regarding teenagers is to do whatever it takes to keep from killing them for a couple of years. Mine actually made it through the tough times in about six months. He is lucky; he was so close!

Too much testosterone or estrogen in too short a period of time makes a kid stupid. You went through the same stuff and you grew out of it. At least I hope you did.

Just bite your tongue. Leave the room. Shut their bedroom door so you do not have to look at their mess. Do whatever it takes. Just keep loving them no matter what they say or do and almost always it will work out okay. Eventually.

CHAPTER 17

Sex:
You Gotta Love It

"Sex is not something we do, it is something we are."
—Mary Calderone

Sex is the coolest thing on the planet and our society has done its best to make it wrong and dirty. We try to legislate it. That does not work. We try to limit it. That does not work. We try to make it appear nasty so people will not want to do it so much. That does not work. In fact, that only makes us want to do it more. So why does none of this work? It is not supposed to. God gave sex to us to enjoy. It is natural. Anything done to inhibit sexual expression will always backfire, because it is a natural thing.

Sexual repression is the cause of many crimes—not sexual expression. Sexual repression is the cause of much guilt—not sexual expression. Sexual repression finances the lives of many psychologists, therapists and writers—not sexual expression. Sexual repression ruins more relationships and marriages than almost any other factor I know of—not sexual expression.

I know you can come up with some exceptions here and so can I.

There are always exceptions, but you must admit I make a very good point.

Think about it. Did you ever hear anyone complain because they were getting too much sex? I did not think so.

Remember the 1960s? I know, I know, some of you do not, but maybe you saw the mini-series or bought the soundtrack. In the 1960s, protesters carried a sign that said, "Make Love, Not War." Know what? They were right.

It is impossible to shoot another person or kill another person while you are having sex. Well, not impossible, but highly unlikely.

So am I saying just go have irresponsible sex with whomever you can? Absolutely not. I say be responsible.

> **"Sex can bring magic into a relationship, and anchor it in a way that no amount of talking or doing things together can."**
>
> —Thomas Moore, *Soul Mates*

Sex is not wrong. Sex is very right. That is the message we should be teaching our children. That is the message we should be telling ourselves every day of our lives. We need to give ourselves permission to enjoy it—in all of its forms.

"Wait! In all of its forms?"

Yes.

"Oh no! You aren't saying. . . ."

Yes.

"But that's wrong."

Who says so?

"God did."

Did She?

"Yes, He did."

Then leave it to God to judge, even though She will not. You stay out of it. Really. Just do the world a favor and butt out. It is none of your business.

Sex with Your Chosen Partner

Make it exciting. Use toys. Have phone sex. Send each other erotic emails. Get some whipped cream and massage oil. Candles and bubble bath are always good. Get creative. Get a good fantasy life going. Talk dirty to each other. Just about anything goes as long as both consent. If it feels good, do it. If you both agree to it, do it. Just enjoy each other.

"But I don't have anyone else to enjoy."

Well, enjoy yourself then.

"?"

You understand.

And remember this about sex: If you are not sweating, you are doing something wrong.

> "Is sex dirty? Only if it's done right."
>
> —Woody Allen

> "We're all so busy acquiring things, when all we really want to do is get naked."
>
> —Jason Purcell

KIDS AND SEX

Abstinence does not work. Do not expect it to. I doubt it worked with you when you were a kid so do not expect it to work with your kids either. It will not. They are going to do it. You probably did. (If not, then it is no wonder you are such a mess!)

"Of all the sexual aberrations, perhaps the most peculiar is chastity."

—Remy de Gourmont

We should teach our kids there is nothing wrong with doing it. It is natural, normal, and as far as I can tell the most fun you are ever going to have—without exception. However, there are guidelines that provide a foundation on which to build every sexual relationship. These are the guidelines that we much teach our kids:

Respect.
Responsibility.
Safety.

These are the three things we should teach our kids about sex. They will figure out what goes where all on their own, but few parents will teach them these three things. Parents and other adults should stop telling kids that sex is bad. It is not. We should stop telling them they are going to ruin their lives by doing it. They are not. Most of all, we should stop telling them they are going to go to hell if they do it. They will not.

My sons lived with their mother growing up, and they attended a large Protestant church that asked them to sign agreements saying they would never engage in sex prior to marriage. Actually this is a common practice in many religious organizations and fundamentalist denominations. And it is nothing but guilt producing. It teaches kids that sex is wrong. And it is not.

All of this guilt-producing teaching has not done one thing to cut back on sexual activity among young adults. It has not cut back on sexual crimes or teenage pregnancy. The only thing I can see it has done is create a society of sexually repressed people who do not understand how to have sex without guilt. Do you find that sad?

So am I condoning premarital sex? Yes. If more couples did it before they got married there would be fewer unhappy marriages and fewer divorces.

Am I saying that kids *should* have sex? No. I am saying that kids *are going* to have sex. Teach them how to do it responsibly. Teach them that no means no—every time and without exception. Educate them about sexually transmitted diseases and about birth control. We ask kids to be responsible and yet we as parents are totally irresponsible when we do not teach our kids how to handle something as powerful as sex.

A good joke—sad, true, but funny:

"Sex is dirty. Save it for someone you love!"

—Dr. Kennedy Shultz

CHAPTER 18

Love Is the Key

Most people would think this chapter on love applies to relationships and should be a part of that chapter. I addressed love in that chapter and have even hinted at it in several others. But love sometimes gets sold a little short when we confine it to the area of relationships. Love is also the key to success, happiness, and prosperity. It is what makes you a great leader, a great salesperson, helps you deliver amazing customer service and makes you the kind of person others want to be with, spend time with, and share their money with.

Who would have thought after all these years that the Beatles were right when they sang, "All you need is love, love, love is all you need?"

Love Is All Powerful

There is no difficulty that enough love will not conquer. There is no disease that enough love will not heal. No door that enough love will not open. No gulf that enough love will not bridge. No wall that enough love will not throw down. And no sin that enough love will not redeem. It makes no difference how deeply seated may be the trouble. How hopeless the outlook. How muddled the tangle. How great the mistake. A sufficient realization of love will dissolve it all. And if you could love enough you would be the happiest and most powerful person in the world.

—Emmet Fox

Fox was right. Love can heal any hurt and fix any problem. Love is *it*. Let me show you.

LOVE WHAT YOU DO

When you love what you do, you will become excellent at it. The more excellent you are at what you do, the more you will be paid to do it. Therefore, loving what you do is the key to your personal compensation and your ultimate prosperity. In addition, when you love what you do, you will be happier, more confident, and even healthier because you are more at ease with your life.

LOVE THOSE YOU DO IT FOR

This means the company you work for as well as the customer who ultimately receives your service. If you do not love the company you work for, then you will not give them your best and will end up cheating them and yourself by withholding the best you have to offer.

Sometimes, businesspeople will pray for more customers, and then when they show up they say, "Lord, I didn't mean *them*!" But those customers, even the ones who drive you crazy, deserve your love. As I have already said, they have the money. Only by loving them enough to serve them well, will they be willing to share their money with you.

LOVE OTHERS

When you love others, sincerely caring about their happiness, then you serve them in the ultimate way. You will show respect, treat them with courtesy, listen to them, encourage them, comfort them, and give them your best. Then all who come in contact with you will want to do the same for you. They will want to extend to you the same love in the same way you have shown them your love. Can you imagine the life you would lead if all who came in contact with you wanted to give you the very best they had to offer?

LOVE YOURSELF

While I have already said this, it bears repeating many times. You cannot be any good for anyone else until you are first good for yourself. I also think it is impossible to really love anyone else unless you first love yourself. How can you give another person your best if you do not believe you have anything wonderful to offer?

LOVE IS THE KEY TO BUSINESS SUCCESS

Love your customers and you will do your very best to serve them well. You will operate honestly in all ways and with integrity. You will price your products and services fairly. You will treat your co-workers with respect. Selling from a motive of love will assure you of reaching your quota. Leading because you love your people will cause them to follow you better than any other tool or tactic. Love will keep the appearance of your business at its best. You will do all of these things because you love what you do and love the people you do it for and do it with. This love will be rewarded. Your customers will reciprocate by loving to do business with you. This means you will be more successful and make more money.

LOVE IS THE KEY TO PROSPERITY

As I have just shown you, love is the key to making more money in business. And as I point out in the chapters on giving and money, sharing your money with others is the key to having more money. But you are only going to be willing to share your wealth when you love the experience of enhancing the lives of others by investing in the lives of others with your cash. Loving to help other people through various charitable organizations will be one of the major factors in guaranteeing your continued financial success.

LOVE IS THE KEY TO HAPPINESS

The end result of every item I have just covered is happiness. I know of no other way to assure a happy life than to extend love to others and to accept the love that comes in return. Your happiness in life will be in direct proportion to the love you give.

> "Love is the law of God. You live that you may learn to love. You love that you may learn to live. No other lesson is required of man."
>
> —Mikhail Naimy

CHAPTER 19

Criticism Happens

There are two kinds of criticism: the kind you give and the kind you get.

Let me first deal with your criticism of others. It is so easy to do, right? And some of it is just natural. You do not like the way someone acted in a certain situation and it bugs you to the point you say something about it. No big deal, in my opinion. That kind of criticism is a normal thing—not a good thing, but not a horrible thing and certainly a normal thing. Then there is the kind of criticism where you say something silly like, "I can't believe she is wearing that!" Again, a natural thing to do and no biggy. These things are not all that bad. Criticism about what someone wears or even what they do is understandable and natural. Criticism becomes dangerous when it is directed about who someone is, not what they do. No one really has the right to talk about who another person is.

"But is that not what you are doing in this book, Larry?"

Not at all. I attack stupidity. I attack laziness. I attack bigotry. I attack hypocrisy. I attack dishonesty. I am not attacking people. I only attack their actions.

A Victim Myself

When I was in my early twenties I had a full beard and hair below my ears. Hard to believe now that I ever had any hair, but that was a long time ago. I worked as one of the first male telephone operators in the country in the small town of Muskogee, Oklahoma, while I was going to college. After graduation, I wanted to transfer to the business office in order to work behind a desk and hopefully move up within the company. I was told I would have to get a haircut and shave my beard. I asked the manager if he was more interested in how much hair I had *on* my head rather than what was *in* my head. The manager said yes, he was. So I shaved. I was much easier to get along with then. Plus, I was pretty much broke and I needed both the job and the money. It is interesting how quickly we will compromise when money is involved.

Do not discount a person's value because you do not like how they look or dress. Do your best to look past all of that. I know it is hard. I am challenged when I go into a retail store and the clerk has purple hair and tattoos from head to toe and a ring through his nose. Or maybe it was her nose. Yet, what I find amazing is that usually I get much better service from someone like that than I do at the big-buck stores where everyone is dressed to the nines.

Try this: If something or someone is not personally hurting you, then mind your own business. If you do not like someone then do not be around him. Do not do business with him. Do not hire him. But do not feel compelled to judge him.

If someone is doing something you do not approve of and it has no effect on your life, then what do you care? Leave her alone. She is choosing to live that way. You get to choose to live your way.

I have discovered what you say about others says more about you than it says about them. Think about the people in your life you cannot stand. What is it about them that you cannot stand? Is that something you cannot stand in yourself? Bet it is.

> **"Everything that irritates us about others can lead us to an understanding of ourselves."**
>
> —Carl Jung

I used to work with a guy who was overbearing, narrow-minded and so outspoken about all of it I could barely stand to be in his presence. I came to realize, however, those are the very things I do not like about me. And it was my irritation with myself over being those ways that made me intolerant of him. What a revelation. What an *uncomfortable* revelation.

I am sure you will find this to be true in your life, too. When you think of the things that irritate you about others, I believe those are the very things you do not like about yourself.

When Others Criticize You

> **"Great spirits have always encountered violent opposition from mediocre minds."**
>
> —Albert Einstein

When you create the life you have always wanted, you will be criticized. I believe that is what Einstein was talking about. People who create the life they have dreamed of are great spirits. They are great spirits because they have dreamed the dream, believed they could accomplish things, and dared to make that life happen. They have set themselves apart from most of society (the mediocre minds) and made something glorious happen. This, by the way, will really bother those who have chosen mediocrity.

Mediocre people will be intimidated by your success. That is because they live in a world steeped in fear and lack. Many of them are convinced if you are successful, then you have used up some of the success that is available for them. You have stolen some of what they could have had if they had only gone after it. They have no idea there is plenty available for all who choose to participate in the abundance that is available for all. They are convinced there is a limited supply and you have taken more than your share. In fact, you have taken part of theirs.

It is not that they do not want you to be successful. It is just that they do not want you to be more successful than they are. These people are also afraid if you become more successful than they, you will move on and leave them behind. You will not be their friend and you will not have time for them. No more wasted afternoons trashing other people; no more extended breaks; no more griping about the high cost of living and whining about how mean and cruel the world is. Actually, that is a valid fear and will probably happen. Once you have become successful you will choose differently. You will not have time for things that move you away from your goal. That includes people who hold you back.

However, the biggest fear people have is fear of themselves. They are afraid they cannot or will not do well, like you have done. They are scared to death to go to the mirror and take responsibility for their lives. And they channel this self-fear into criticism of you.

So they will criticize you to your face and behind your back. They will make little jokes about how you are moving up. They will try to get others to side with them, and sadly some will do it. Even Jesus said, "The poor will be with you always." The best thing you can do for the poor is to not be one of them. You cannot change these people. You cannot even bring them with you. All people must follow their own path. Learn to live with it. Love them, bless them, and let them go.

"So long as you are still worried about what others think of you, you are owned by them."
— Neale Donald Walsch,
Conversations with God, Book 3

Do not bother defending your success. You have nothing to defend. You took advantage of your talents and abilities. You went to work on yourself and on your life and now you are reaping the benefits. You did well as a result of serving others well. You have been rewarded for the service you have provided. You deserve everything you have. You did it. Just you. Do not apologize for it. Do not be embarrassed by it. Simply be thankful and enjoy it. You can only achieve true happiness when you rise above the approval of others.

"If you know with a complete absence of doubt that what you are doing is consistent with your own purpose and that you are involved in accomplishing a great affair, then you are at peace with yourself and in harmony with your own heroic mission."
— Dr. Wayne Dyer

A guaranteed way to avoid criticism:

"Say nothing. Do nothing. Be nothing."
— Unknown

Cynicism versus Criticism

Cynicism is much different than criticism. I believe cynicism is actually a good thing. If people had a little more cynicism we would not have had the Branch Davidians, or the mass suicides surrounding Jim Jones, or all of the people being duped by Jim Bakker and his kind, or the issues the Catholics are facing with their priests right now. Blind trust is a dangerous thing. We must question everything: religion, God, authority, politicians, the government, academia, medicine, laws, . . . everything. The things that stand up to close, cynical scrutiny are the things you can best believe in and count on. If things fall apart when looked at, then they had little value in the first place.

By the way, I did mean to include God in that statement. God can handle your cynicism and questioning—religion, on the other hand, may not tolerate it.

Here is good thing to remind yourself: Your cynicism will be confused with criticism. I have discovered the majority of the people in this world do not understand the difference between cynicism and criticism. You will be judged as a critic when you do not take things at face value. People will consider you mean and negative and a troublemaker. Rise above it. Just smile and know you are not a sucker— you just asked about something before you accepted it as truth.

And one more thing: When you voice your cynicism, gauge the reaction to what you have to say. If there is a hostile reaction to your questioning, your ideas, your thoughts and your cynicism, then beware of those who argue the loudest. The truth does not care if it is questioned; the truth can always stand up to questioning. I have found that only the false fights back, retaliates, and attacks. The truth might defend itself, though it does not really need to. But liars trying to defend their lies get mean and dirty.

CHAPTER 20

The More You Give the More You Get

We spend most of our lives trying to figure out how to get more when the answer is so easy. You get more by giving more. Yes, it is as simple as that. You get by giving. That is the irony.

You get to the proper weight by giving up the foods that are not good for you. You get success by giving up all of the things that keep you from being successful. Things like too much television, lousy work habits, and being lazy.

See how it works? That is how you get more money, too. Give some of the money you have.

GIVING MONEY

"Give freely, joyously, lovingly, and with a sense of abandonment, and as you do, fabulous wealth inevitably will be yours."

—Joseph Murphy

Feed the children; feed the homeless; save the whales; save the rain forest. Mothers Against Drunk Driving; AIDS research; United Way; Jerry's Kids—and on and on. Every one of these causes and all of the others in the world could be financed and most of the problems solved if people would do some giving and stop talking about doing some giving.

You hear people say what a shame it is we have children who are starving right here in America. They are right, it is. It is a shame to have anyone starving anywhere. So how much have you given to bring an end to the problem? Really—how much? Give me a dollar amount. When did you give it? How long ago? When was the last time you actually sat down and put pen to check and gave a nice chunk of change to solve even one of the world's problems?

Most people talk about all the good that needs to be done, and so few do anything about it. It is just talk. Talk does not fix much. I know: I sell talk.

Money Fixes Stuff

I grew up a foot-washing fundamentalist. One of the old gospel songs I heard growing up was, *"You're so heavenly-minded you're no earthly good."* What a great thing for all of us to remember. Our thoughts are so lofty—so full of love—so full of willingness to do anything within our power to help. Anything but write a check.

Some people do give; I will grant you that. If you are one of the few who do, then I applaud you. But most do not give. How can they justify that? Is it because they do not have enough to give? Hardly. Everyone has enough to give something. It is not because they do not have it. It comes down to the fact they will not give it.

Why? Are they afraid they will diminish their supply by giving part of it away? Actually just the opposite is true. The more you give of what you have, the more you actually get. It is the coolest thing. I tried to figure that out for a long time until I discovered it was actually one of the Laws of Physics.

Nature Abhors a Vacuum

It is only when you give things away that you make room for more. And it is usually better stuff!

Try this: Go to your closet. Go to the bad end. Women, you know exactly what I am talking about when I say the bad end. Men, you probably do not have a clue which is the bad end because for most men, both ends and the middle are bad. So ask a woman, a gay friend, or me for help with this one. Now that you have identified the bad end, pull out all of the clothes hanging there. Things you will never wear again which have been out of style for years, and things you could not begin to get your fat butt in any longer. Now give it away. Do not argue with me—just give it away. Do not take it to a re-sale shop for a couple of bucks—do not have a garage sale—just give it to an organization that can really use it.

"But I won't have anything left to wear!"

Good. Now you will have to replace it, with better stuff that you like, that is in fashion and fits.

Look at your sofa. Hate it? Put it on the curb in front of your house with a sign that says, "Free." Within two hours it will disappear. Within two weeks you will have replaced it.

And this is the cool part: giving to those who actually need what you are getting rid of will help create the abundance necessary to re-place it.

"The secret of prosperity is generosity, for by sharing with others the good that life gives us we open up the wellsprings of abundance."

—J. Donald Walters

"A man there was they called him mad. The more he gave the more he had."

—John Bunyan

CHAPTER 21

Sometimes Work Is Just Plain Work

No way to avoid it—work is a part of everyone's life. You have to work. I have not figured out a way to avoid it. Some have. Those are not people you want to emulate, however. Work is a given, not just because it is the major source of your income but also because it is the major source of both your personal and professional fulfillment and inner satisfaction.

I have already talked about the importance of loving what you do. However, to those who say, "just love what you do and you will never work a day in your life"—I say bull! Those people are idiots. No matter how much you love what you do, sometimes it is work! And sometimes it will not be fun. And sometimes you will hate it. Even if what you do is the true fulfillment of all the creative and fun energy you have in your heart, mind, body, and soul, sometimes you will get tired of it and hate it. That is reality.

I love what I do. I travel to great places, stay in great hotels, eat in great restaurants, for the most part deal with pretty nice people and get paid well for doing it. I get to say just about anything I want to say and I get to be myself. Yet sometimes, I hate it. I get ill thinking about having to crawl on one more airplane, having to sleep in one more hotel room, and having to eat one more room service cobb salad. Does it mean I do not love what I do for a living? Not at all. I do love it. And I would not trade it for any other profession. It only means I am tired. But I'm not tired of doing what I really do, which is to speak. I am sometimes tired of everything that goes with the speaking—the travel, dealing with airports and hotels and rental car companies, being away from home and missing my wife, dog, friends, family and my stuff—tired of all that is a part of what I do but not really what I do, which is the time I spend on the platform.

That is the reality of work. You only really do what you do a small percentage of the time. In fact, if you look at just about any profession, you wind up actually doing the profession about 10 percent of the time, and the other 90 percent of the time you do the things that support the 10 percent.

For instance, in a sales job you only spend about 10 percent of your time actually selling. The other 90 percent is spent traveling to or from appointments, making phone calls, placing orders, going to meetings, talking to other departments, filling out paperwork and many other things that have little to do with actual selling. Can you get out of it? I doubt it. It comes with the territory. Do you like it? Maybe, maybe not. It doesn't really matter whether you like it—it is just part of the deal.

It really does not matter much what you do for a living; you will find that very little time is spent doing it. Are you a plumber? How much time do you actually spend with tools in your hand? My guess is about 10 percent. Are you a piano tuner? How much time do you spend in front of a piano? About 10 percent. Are you a manager? How much of your time is actually spent managing? About 10 percent.

What is my point? Love the 10 percent of what you do and put up with the other 90 percent. You are still paid and rewarded primarily for the 10 percent.

I recognize this is not a profound, lofty idea—I do not do those. This is an idea based on reality. Work is work. And many times work sucks. Face it. Deal with it. Make the best of it. Love the parts of it you can and just suck it up and deal with the rest of it.

A Helpful Idea

While work is sometimes work, I do believe it is important for us to understand why we go to work every day. I believe that knowing the *why* helps us deal with the *how*. So I am going to give you the why you go to work every day:

Three Reasons You Go to Work Every Single Day

1. To keep existing customers.
2. To create new customers.
3. To make yourself and your organization the kind that other people want to do business with.

That is it. Those are the reasons you go to work every single day. Of course, I know many of you will immediately reject these reasons by saying you do not have customers, but you do. Everyone has customers. You might call them something else, but you still have customers. You might call them clients. In the medical community, you would call them patients. In education, students. In my world, the audience. You might also call them co-workers or employees. The thing to remember is this: Your job requires you to serve others. Even if you are the boss, you must serve your employees. As Bob Dylan sang, "You gotta serve somebody." Bob was right. All of us have to serve somebody. And in business, I call that "somebody" the customer.

THE FIRST REASON: TO KEEP EXISTING CUSTOMERS

The lifeblood of any organization is its existing customer base. These are the people who are already doing business with you—the people who know you, trust you, and have paid you for your services. Keeping them is your primary reason for going to work each day. You want repeat business. You need repeat business. You want these people to know you, love you, and to tell their friends about you. And these good people who have done business with you and who keep coming back to you are the people who will forgive you when you make a mistake, because you will make a mistake. We all do. They will forgive you because they know you can do better and have done better in the past. When shown some appreciation, these customers and their loyalty can help you survive the toughest of times and help you prosper during the best of times. They are your best friends. Treat them right!

THE SECOND REASON: TO CREATE NEW CUSTOMERS

Some people think this should actually be the number one reason for going to work. Many have argued this point with me but I can assure you they are wrong. Creating new customers cannot be first; it must be second. Did you ever see a company that neglected existing customers in order to pursue new customers? When that happens, those existing customers will go someplace else and become new customers for a new company. How sad. Those customers belonged to a company that blew it by either ignoring them or by treating them poorly. So the customers went elsewhere.

That is probably how you got your new customers—someone else did not treat them right. Now it is your turn to get new customers and all you really have to do is treat them right. You do not have to be cheaper and sometimes you do not even have to be better than your competition. You just have to treat people better.

Then once those customers have done business with you, they become your existing customers and it is your chance to treat them well so they will not go elsewhere again.

THE THIRD REASON: TO MAKE YOURSELF AND YOUR ORGANIZATION THE KIND THAT OTHER PEOPLE WANT TO DO BUSINESS WITH

This is actually the toughest reason of all. The other reasons are primarily based on your activities. This one is based on the kind of person you are. And when you add together the combined personalities and values of all who work at your business, you come up with an organization that has a personality and a set of values. The values and personality of any organization is only a reflection of the values and personality of its individual employees' personalities. Got it? And it does not matter what the plaques on the walls say. I have gone into many businesses that put big banners and plaques on the wall proclaiming how they feel about their customers. This stuff is proudly displayed so all customers will know exactly how the company feels about them. The problem is that they forgot to tell the employees. Yet, customers do not do business with companies, they do business with the employees of the company. That is where the belief in customers must start—with the people who have direct contact with the customers.

Ever had to get your driver's license renewed? Or get a new license plate for your car? I will bet the minute you walked into the Department of Motor Vehicles you got an overwhelming feeling that said, "This is not going to be a pleasant experience." The very air in the room screamed that at you. All businesses scream at you.

It usually is not as noticeable as it is when you enter a government-run organization, but it exists.

So evaluate your company. What feeling do your customers get about you and your organization when they do business with you? Do your customers get the feeling you really care about their satisfaction? Or do they get the feeling they are just one more bozo that has to be put up with until it is time to go home? It really is up to you.

SOME SHORT LESSONS ABOUT WORK

When you work, work! When you play, play! Do not mix the two. It only screws up the work *and* the play. This is especially true if you work at home. Be able to walk away. I have a home office. Many people have home offices these days. Sadly, many people are good at having a home office. They just do not get much work done. Or even more sadly, they do not get much living done. You must be able to walk away from "home" and its duties and responsibilities to go to "work" and take on those duties and responsibilities. More important, you have to be able to walk away from the work and live your life. It is hard for some people.

Make your work area a place where you only do work things. Do not eat at your desk or do any personal things at your desk. When you are not working, stay away from that area. If your work area has a door, then close it. If it does not have a door, put one in! Close off the area where you work from the place where you rest, relax, and play.

Be Known for the Right Stuff.   You have a reputation. You may not have wanted a reputation and you probably did not expect to have one, but it still exists. You may be known as the office joker, the guy with bad breath, or the office slut—and sadly, it does not matter if it is true. It is your reputation. I suggest you try to create a reputation before one is assigned to you. And my suggestion is that you be known as the person who gets things done.

I have a reputation for being an asshole. I can assure you it is a well-earned reputation. I do what I can to perpetuate it. However, the reputation of being a pain to work with did not come about because I lie, am dishonest, do not deliver a high-quality product, show up late, am discourteous, or am lazy. My reputation is because I do what I say I am going to do when I said I would, and I refuse to compromise quality or ethics for any reason. I will not be late and I will not tolerate anyone else being late. I will not lie and I will not tolerate being lied to. I deliver the best possible product I can to the best of my ability every time and I expect the same from those who do business with me. This makes me a total pain to do business with because I have a standard by which I perform and I expect those who do business with me to perform to the same standard. Because of this, I am known as an asshole. Better to get this reputation for the right reasons instead of the wrong reasons.

Get the Hard Stuff out of the Way First.   It is kind of like being a little kid and having to clean your plate. If you are smart, you learn to eat the broccoli first and save the macaroni and cheese for later. The same applies to work. Do the stuff that is not your favorite when you first get there. Do not put it off. Just get it done, get it out of the way, and move on to the stuff you enjoy.

Stay Focused.   Do one job until completion when at all possible. Figure out the most important thing that has to be done today. Then do it. If it really has to be done, you will have accomplished something meaningful regardless of what else does not get done. Focus on things of real importance and let the less important things slide. No one ever gets in trouble for doing the things that really matter. The things that really matter produce results that really matter, and we are all measured on the quality of our results, not the quality of our activities.

When It Quits Being Fun, Quit.   This was discussed in detail in Chapter 7 but you need to be reminded of it again here. If you honestly hate your job, then you either need to learn again to fall in love with parts of it, or you need to move on to a different job. There is no way to be excellent at something you do not enjoy.

SOME SHORT LESSONS ABOUT BUSINESS

Do not make it your goal to be the cheapest. Make it your goal to be the best. People who only shop price are not good customers. Companies that sell only on price are rarely good companies to buy from. Anyone can offer you a product or service for a nickel less. And any company can lower their price. But when you give up money, you give up something else: quality, service, or a piece of your integrity. Do not underestimate the customer's willingness to pay more in order to get more. Piece of mind, confidence, buyer satisfaction, and pride in ownership are worth money that many are willing to pay.

Treat People Better Than You Are Willing to be Treated. The golden rule is wrong. Do not just treat people the way you want to be treated. Treat them better. Your level of expectation might be pretty low. My expectation when doing business with others is sometimes very low. (I go to restaurants and if the food even shows up, I have a party.) Therefore, you might be willing to accept a lower quality of service than your customer is willing to accept. Do not judge what others want by what you are willing to accept. Err on the side of more. Give more than they expect. Be nicer than they expect. Give better service than they expect. Surprise people by going the extra mile.

You Cannot Get a Good Deal from a Bad Guy.   This is a biggy. I have tried to get a good deal from a bad guy and it just cannot be done. Bad people became bad because they do bad things. Do not fall victim to thinking you can be the one person who is going to get a good deal. And if you try but get burned, it is your fault, not theirs. I once tried to sell a guy a house and when we signed the deal, it did not feel right. He had a smarmy feel about him. But I was desperate to sell. Sure enough, the deal fell apart, I lost money and it got ugly. I learned a couple of lessons. First, follow your gut. If the deal does not feel right, do not do it. Second, a snake will always try to bite you. Do not blame the snake—it is only following its nature. Blame yourself for being willing to get close to it.

Friends and Family Pay Full Retail.   When I was in the business of selling telephone systems, a friend of mine asked me to bid on installing a new system in his office. I gave him the price and then because he was my very good friend, I offered him a discount. He politely turned it down and said he wanted to pay full retail. I asked him why and he told me if he paid full retail, if there were a problem he would have paid for the right to complain. If he got a discount, he forfeited that right. I learned a great lesson that day. By the way, you can use this line when doing business with friends or family. Tell them you want to reserve for them the right to gripe about the service or the product by paying full retail.

The Number One, Most Important, Get-This-or-Fail Short Lesson for Both Work and Business.   Do what you say you are going to do, when you said you were going to do it, in the way you said you were going to do it. No excuses. No pointing the finger of blame elsewhere. No nothing! Just keep your word. Period. Be the person your co-workers and your customers can put their trust, faith, and confidence in—without exception.

Do what you say you are going to do,

when you said you were going to do it,

in the way you said you were going to do it.

CHAPTER 22

You Are
Out of Time

"There is just no time!!!"

Well, for once we almost agree on something. There is not much time. And it seems there is less time every day. I am a victim of this one just like you. I need more time. I want more time. There is too much to do and not enough time to do it.

What to do, what to do? I know! Go to a time management seminar. Or buy an organizer and carry it with you all the time so you can plot and plan every moment of every day. Those things will work. Yeah, right!

Time Management Is a Joke

Saying that always upsets my friends who teach time management. Good. They are wrong for attempting to teach you how to manage your time. Time cannot be managed. Stop trying. It will only frustrate you. Forget about having the time or not having the time. There is nothing you can do to get more of it anyway, so give it up. Different approach, huh?

Instead of focusing on how much time you have, or do not have or need to have, begin to focus on what your priorities are. The problem is never a lack of time; the problem is poorly defined priorities. When you have established the most important thing in the world for you to do, then time will take care of itself.

If I came to your house, opened your garage door and began to look at your messy garage, like most people you would probably say you have been meaning to clean the place but you have just been too busy. Yeah, wrong. You have not been too busy at all. You did not clean your garage because it was not a priority to you. If it had been a priority you would have found the time to clean it. Our priorities almost always get done because we find and make the time for them. On the other hand, the things that are not all that important to us we let slide.

This idea applies to every area of your life. If I gave you a book that if read and the principles implemented, would guarantee you more success, money and happiness in your life, would you read it? If you are this far, then the answer is yes. But do you actually know why you are reading it? Are you reading this book because there is nothing else you could be doing? No. You are reading it because it is a priority to you. You actually have made success, happiness, and prosperity priorities and are now doing something to make those things happen.

Funny how even though you are a busy person—and I know you are—you were able to either find the time or make the time to read this book. Other people say they want more success, happiness, and prosperity and they will never find the time to read this book. Even though they may have bought the book, they will still not read it. Not this book or any other one. And their excuse will be they have just not had the time to do it. Why? Success, happiness, and prosperity are not priorities to them. Watching *Survivor* or *Everybody Loves*

Raymond or *Seinfeld* reruns—those were their priorities. They found the time to watch TV but did not find the time to read a book. And they wonder why they are not doing well? Doing well is not a priority to them.

Too busy to clean the garage? To play with your kids? To read a book? To call your mom? To go to a movie or to dinner with your spouse? How about if I called and offered you a round of golf at the best course in town for free? Would you be too busy for that? If you were a golfer, you would find the time. You would make the time, because that round of golf would have become a priority to you.

ESTABLISH PRIORITIES

Do you have things in your life that need to be done—things that you really want to see accomplished—yet you just have not been able to find the time to get them done? Right now face the fact those things are never going to get done until they become a priority to you. Figure out what is really important to you. In other words, establish priorities.

Is it your health? If it is, then you will *know* it is when you do things that make you healthier like eating a proper diet and exercising regularly. Nothing will stand in your way. Not your work, your favorite television show, or any other excuse. There will be enough time for you to get healthy because you will make enough time to get healthy.

Is your priority to spend more time with your family? If it is, then you will *know* it is when you really begin to make time for them. Nothing will stand in your way.

Face the facts. In the normalcy of life sometimes the things you do not want to do have to be your priority. Things like picking up the kids, meeting the repairman, and accomplishing your list of honey-do's. I would rather take a beating than meet a repairman. They are never on time and rarely call to advise they will be late; they usually have to come back a second time because they do not have the right things with them to do the job the first time. All of that drives me insane! Yet, life dictates that I sometimes have to do it. Been there? Suck it up. That is my only advice. Sorry, no sage philosophy on this one. Just suck it up and do what it takes to get the job done.

Life is full of have-to's. There is no way around it. I have them. You have them—things that we are not wild about doing but still have to do. Welcome to life. The key is to figure out how to get them done and still have time to do what you want to do, right?

Just please stop saying there is not enough time. There is plenty of time. Time to take care of the stupid things that have to be done. Besides, it is not the stupid things that are keeping you from having the time to accomplish what you want to accomplish. It is all of the things you let creep into your life because you do not have clearly defined priorities.

There is plenty of time to do what is really important to you. Stop being frustrated. Yes, time is short and as we age, it seems to get shorter. But there will never be enough time to do everything there is to do. However, there is plenty of time to do the things you really want to do. If you want it badly enough you will find the time or make the time.

DO NOT WATCH YOUR WATCH

I love watches. I have several. But I think of them more as jewelry than as timepieces. One reason is that when I hit 50, I could not see the watch face too well so I rarely knew what time it was anyway. And the little date window on the watch face? What a joke! The most important reason I do not pay that much attention to my watch any longer is something my dad said many times as I was growing up: "We do not wear a watch to know what time it *is*, we wear a watch to know what time it *isn't.*" He was so right! Do you really ever care what time it is? Now hold on; do not answer too quickly. Do not start yelling, "Well, of course I do! I have appointments, planes to catch, things to do, people to see." Big deal—we all do. How busy you are does not impress me or anyone else. So hang on and let me explain. Do you look at your watch to see if it is time to leave for your appointment or to see if it is not yet time to leave for your appointment? I bet it is the latter. We do not care what time it *is*, we only care what time it is not. It is not time to go to lunch. It is not time to go to the airport. It is not time for bed. It is not time to go to work.

And if it is not time to do those things, there must still be time to do something else. That is what you really want, right? Time to do something else. Time enough to get another cup of coffee. Time enough to relax a little longer. Time to do what you want to do instead of what you have to do.

So what time *is* it? Time to do the most important thing that needs to be done.

> **If the most important thing gets done,**
> **regardless of what it is,**
> **nothing else really matters much.**

CHAPTER 23

Success Is
a Balancing Act

Years ago I came up with my personal definition of success: Success is being all you can be in each area of your life without sacrificing your ability to be all you can be in each and every other area of your life. This definition is based in balance. It makes no sense to be the world's greatest salesperson and have bad health. It is nothing but sad to have made a lot of money but sacrificed your family along the way. Never sacrifice one area over another. I believe as Tom Hopkins once said, "To be rich and sick is stupid."

While I am a firm believer in balance, I am also very realistic regarding balance and the achievement of success in the various areas of life. In order to achieve balance, you must first become unbalanced. In other words, if you are broke and need money, then you are going to have to become unbalanced in order to make that happen. You are not going to have the time to relax, or play with the family quite as much or work out as much. You have to work. I understand that. I even condone that. For a while. Not for long, though. At some point you still have to go back to paying attention to all the other areas of life. That is the challenge. It seems when we focus on our work, we lose perspective and let the other areas of life suffer. Then we become accustomed to not seeing our kids or playing with them, and we get used to not taking care of ourselves physically. And before you know it, you have no relationship with your family and you are sick and tired and lonely and old. Yeah, you are rich and you have a big office, but that is about it. Be careful. Work hard but not so hard you lose your life.

It works the other way around, too. Play hard. But do not play so hard that you sacrifice your livelihood either. Balance is the key. Think of your life in terms of a wheel with spokes. Each spoke represents the various areas of your life: physical, intellectual, spiritual, social, financial, career, family, fun and play, alone time, friends, and civic responsibility. With each of these areas as the spoke of a wheel, considering your own life, how smooth is the ride? Do all of the spokes hit the ground on a regular basis? Or do you have some flat spots?

Growth in one area of your life means you will let another area slide slightly. But *slightly* is the operative word. Do not completely abandon any one area in pursuit of another. People who do that, and I am sure you can name a few, are one-dimensional, boring, and end up leading sad, unfulfilled lives. They have cheated themselves, those around them, and the rest of the world by not living life to its fullest in all areas.

CHAPTER 24

Give Up Hope

You have been told the virtues of having hope for nearly your entire life. You have heard it said that sometimes having hope is the only thing you can have when facing a crisis. I believe having hope is a waste of time. Yeah, yeah—blasphemy again! What I just said flies in the face of all you hold holy, right? But I will not back down. I am telling you to give up hope. Hope has never done you a bit of good.

Hope says you wish something would happen the way you want it to, but it could just as easily not happen. Hope is grounded in uncertainty.

Instead of Hope, Have Faith

Faith is grounded in absolute certainty. Faith is a "knowing." Without a doubt you know something is true and you can count on it. I know the sun will come up tomorrow. I have faith in it. I know there is a

God and that God wants the best for me: health, prosperity, success, and happiness. I have faith in it and I can count on it.

Having that certainty gives me the courage to act. I am willing to act on anything when certainty is involved. I am much more hesitant when doubt is involved. I bet you are the same way. You should forget hope and doubt and instead have faith and certainty, and then step out boldly.

CHAPTER 25

Guilt Serves
No Purpose

"But what am I supposed to feel when I do something I am sorry for?"

Good question. Easy answer: regret.

It is natural to have some regret when you have made a mistake. That is not guilt. We all make mistakes and feel bad about it. That is regret. Regret means you are sorry and you do not want to repeat the same action again. Good. Guilt is the emotion that immobilizes you. That is why guilt serves no purpose. It will not help you in any way. It is a waste of time. You cannot change what has been done by feeling guilty about it.

The past is just that: passed. Gone. Slipped away. Not to be repeated again. If you need to make restitution, do it. If you messed up, apologize. If you are forgiven for your mistake, give thanks and move on. If you are not forgiven for the mistake you made, then move on anyway. Forgive yourself, learn from the experience, and act differently next time. At that point, it is over.

CHAPTER 26

Worry Is
a Waste of Time

There are only two areas of life: the things you can control and the things you cannot control. Why worry about what you cannot control? How stupid is that? If you *can* control it, then why worry about it? After all, it is in your control, thus making worry a total waste of energy.

The past is something you cannot control. It is over. Do not worry about it. The future is something you can control. But do not worry about it either. Just do something about it. The present is also in your control. Live it the way you want to live it and know you should live it, and it will take care of itself—worry will only turn it in a direction you do not want it to take.

This is a hard thing to do. I know it is. My son was in Baghdad during Operation Iraqi Freedom. I hated it. Like all of the families of our men and women in the service, I was scared to death for him. I did not agree with the war and did not want my son there fighting. But there was not one thing I could do about it. It was his job. A job he enjoyed and had volunteered to do so it was beyond my control. My worry about him did him no good and it was wrecking my life. So

I reminded myself of my own credo to forget worry. Worry is a misuse of your imagination. Worry attracts to you exactly what you do not want to happen. Like Job says in the Bible, "For the thing which I greatly feared is come upon me, and that which I was afraid of is come unto me" (Job 3:25 KJV). Because I know this to be true about worry, I gave it up. Instead I turned my energy toward him coming home safely. I put my energy into the outcome I wanted, instead of the outcome I did not want.

Stop focusing on what you do not want to happen. In other words, stop worrying. Instead, stay focused on what you want to happen. The attention you give that thing will attract it to you. Trust me, this is a cosmic thing. Focus your energy on the kind of life you want, the relationship you want, the stuff you want, and the way you want to feel. This will work for anything. Focus and you will draw to you exactly what you really want. And it works in reverse. Look at what you have—every condition of your life. You have that condition in your life because that was your focus. Change your focus and you will change your results.

"The secret of success is constancy of purpose."
—Benjamin Disraeli

CHAPTER 27

Selfishness
Is a Good Thing

You have been told your whole life not to be selfish, but the people who told you that were dead wrong. You should share your money and your stuff and your talents—I have already addressed that. However, you have to learn to be selfish with yourself. Your first obligation is to yourself. You cannot be any good for someone else unless you are first good to yourself.

> "Betrayal of yourself in order not to betray another is betrayal nonetheless. It is the highest betrayal."
> —Neale Donald Walsch,
> *Conversations with God*, Book 3

Being selfish is actually a form of service. When you do what you love to do and enjoy doing, only then are you going to be excellent at it and serve others better. You will be rewarded for it and serve yourself and family better. It will also give you more in life for you to share. Selfishness is actually the path to unselfishness.

Be selfish with your time. Learn to say no to things you do not want to do and have no interest in. You are not serving anyone when you spread yourself too thin. Say no to the things that keep you from saying yes to what you really want to do in life. That way, the things you say yes to will get your full attention, and you will do a better job at those things and end up serving everyone, including yourself, much better.

Be selfish with your help. Am I saying to stop being helpful? Absolutely not. I am just saying to give your help wholeheartedly to those who want it, but selfishly to those who need it. Many people need help—we all recognize that. But many of those who need help just do not want it. So do not help them. People who need help rarely appreciate it when it is given, and rarely do anything with the help anyway. Do not waste your time. Instead, help people who sincerely want to be helped. They will appreciate it and actually use the help given them. Help as many people as you possible can, but only those who want to be helped. It is more fulfilling to you and more beneficial for those who receive it.

CHAPTER 28

A Deal
Is a Deal

This is an old saying I know you have heard many times, so whatever happened to living up to it?

Remember the movie *Indecent Proposal* with Robert Redford, Demi Moore, and Woody Harrelson? Redford offers $1 million to spend one night with Demi (not a bad investment if you ask me). Demi and Woody are newlyweds with money problems and agree to take the $1 million, and off she trots to spend the night with Redford (not a bad deal for Demi, if you ask my wife). Then poor old Woody goes ape! Hey Woody, a deal is a deal. Grow up.

We have all made mistakes of overpromising—your mouth often overloads your ass, as the saying goes. So? What difference should that make? What does any of it have to do with the fact that you made a commitment and now are expected to live up to it? So you over-promised and now are not happy about it. A deal is a deal. Suck it up and keep your word.

Yes, it might cost you some money to live up to your word. Yes, it might be painful to deliver on your promise. Yes, it might be embar-rassing to you or humiliate you. It might be expensive or inconvenient.

Tough! A deal is a deal. Make a better deal *next* time—be smarter *next* time—but *this* time live up to your commitment.

If you make a promise, keep it. If you give your word, do not go back on it. If you say you are going to be there at a certain time, be there. If you mess up, admit it and accept the consequences. If you are paid for a service, provide that service when you said you would and exactly as you said you would. Any less than this makes you a liar. Harsh? Too bad. I told you I was going to be harsh, and after all: A deal is a deal.

CHAPTER 29

Hard Lessons to Learn

These are the short lessons that are sometimes hard to learn and hard to accept. They do not need a chapter to explain them. They do not even need a paragraph. They just need to be stated, understood, and accepted.

■ When people tell you how rich they are, chances are they are not.

■ When people tell you how intelligent they are, they actually are proving how little they know, not how much they know.

■ When people tell you how successful they are, chances are they are not.

■ When people tell you what a devout Christian they are, especially more than once, they are usually anything but.

■ When people tell you how honest they are, keep your hand on your wallet.

■ When people say, "let me be frank with you," it means in the past they have not been.

■ When people say, "and that's the truth," be skeptical.

■ When people say, "let me tell you this for your own good," it is for their own good, not yours.

■ When people say, "I only have one thing to say about that," be prepared for a lot more than one thing to follow.

■ When people say, "I'll try," do not count on it.

Things like honesty, integrity, Christianity, intelligence, success, and most other good things do not need to be said or bragged about or crammed down someone's throat. They show. You do not even have to talk about them. They are just there. Proof is always in the action, not the words. Actions say what you believe and the kind of person you are much more than your words. Results are everything and they never lie.

More Hard Lessons

■ Never say anything stupid like, "It just can't get any worse than this!" That is a challenge you do not want to issue to the Universe. If there is one thing I have learned in life, it is that it can *always* get worse.

■ There is an old saying that goes, "Kids should be seen and not heard." Actually I think the truer statement would be, "Neighbors should be seen and not heard."

■ Rich makes up for a whole lot of ugly.

■ The less people have to say, the more they feel compelled to say it.

■ Common sense is no longer common. Neither is common knowledge or common courtesy.

■ When someone says, "If I had a nickel for every time . . ." the truth is they would have about 35 cents.

CHAPTER 30

The Test
for Success

At this point you probably want to know, "If I do all of this stuff, will I be successful?"

Yes, if you do all of this stuff I believe you will be successful. However, I have put together a little test for you to take. This test will tell you whether you have achieved success better than any other test I have ever come across.

Am I happy?
Am I healthy?
Am I serving?
Am I loving?
Am I learning?
Am I having fun?
Am I doing something I enjoy?
Am I prosperous?

If the answer to each of these questions is yes, then celebrate — you are successful.

If the answer to any of these questions is no, then stop and do whatever it takes to turn that no into a yes.

A Few Words of Caution

Success does not mean that you will not have problems or bumps in the road. If you believe that is the way it is, then you are truly naive. Life is just not like that, and actually I do not believe you would really want it to be. Life is more like riding a rollercoaster. I like to ride the rollercoaster. It has its uphill climbs that chug-chug-chug along and fill you with anticipation. It has its downhill runs at breakneck speeds that will terrify you. It has dark, scary tunnels where you scream and become so afraid that you might even cry. There is something not quite completely safe about rollercoasters. They feel dangerous. Sometimes you even throw up! But for the most part they leave you laughing hysterically and grabbing the person next to you out of joy and fear and a rush of many emotions.

A rollercoaster is never dull. When you get off, you cannot wait to get back on and do it again. So you either pay the price of admission and go along for the ride, or you spend your life as an observer, watching the others have all the fun. Or you spend your time waiting in line, and then when it is finally your turn, you step back to let someone else go on ahead of you because you are not sure you can handle the ride. Some even choose to just skip the rollercoaster altogether and instead get on the merry-go-round where the sweet music plays and you go around in circles. It is nice and safe, the music is good, and it is a pleasant experience for all. You were never afraid and you never cried and you never threw up. But you never screamed with laughter and you never cried out in terror and you never grabbed the person next to you out of joy or for comfort.

I have done the merry-go-round and I have ridden the roller-coaster. I have made my choice. I choose the rollercoaster. There is more risk when you choose the rollercoaster, but at least you will know you have lived.

Answering yes to the questions on the test proves not only that you are living, but that you are living a life of purpose, fulfillment, and enjoyment.

CHAPTER 31

A Final Thought

You are finished. You have read the book. Good for you, you are now further along than most people will ever be. But are you really finished? Hardly. All you have done is finish the book. Now is when the hard stuff happens for you, because now you have to take some action.

I hope you will take action. I hope you will choose to live life differently. Maybe for you it will be only slightly different, and maybe because of where you are it will be drastically different. But the key is it takes movement for things to change—a movement in the way you think, talk, and act.

Let me close with a question I was recently asked by a magazine reporter, and my response.

He asked: "At the end of the day, what really matters?"

My answer: "Not much. Really, not much matters. At the end of the day if you smiled more than you frowned, laughed more than you cried, told your family and friends you loved them, and had a pretty good time doing what you do for a living, then it was a good day. Go to bed and say thanks."

If you do not do the stuff I have suggested in this book, it is fine with me. I do not know you and will not know if you do it or not. My real goal for you is in the answer I gave the reporter. Make that your goal. If you can do those things, you are okay in my books.

> **"Those are my principles, and if you don't like them, I have more."**
>
> **—Groucho Marx**